The Descendants Of John I Yeoman, Of Moss Side, Near Yealand Redman, Lancashire

Joseph Foster

Alpha Editions

This Edition Published in 2021

ISBN: 9789354413964

Design and Setting By
Alpha Editions
www.alphaedis.com
Email - info@alphaedis.com

CONTENTS.

PORTRAIT GROUPS.

PREFACE.

THIS genealogical record of a prominent Quaker family and its collaterals is yet another testimony to the spiritual force and marvellous vitality of the teaching of George Fox. The history of the house is co-extensive with that of the Society of Friends, which was joined by its founder, a simple yeoman, one of that class which contributed so largely, in the seventeenth century, to the making not only of England, but of the United States of America. The spirit of the Pilgrim Fathers in the "Mayflower," and of the "Ironsides" on the field of battle, fighting for liberty of conscience, was also shown in that of the Friends when, "in their resolute performance of duties they conceived imposed upon them," they faced every hardship in the sacred cause of toleration. It was reflected in that sturdy yeoman, John Backhouse (p. 13), who, in 1661, endured patiently months of imprisonment in Lancaster Castle for meeting to worship with other Friends. In 1684 his cattle were sold for payment of tithes, and his younger son, James Backhouse (p. 14), our ancestor, obtained a place in Friends' "Book of Sufferings," by dying a prisoner in the same place and for the same cause in 1697. With unflinching persistence the family have adhered to the principles for which he died, and have continued to oppose as sturdily, even unto the present day, the similar impost of church rates.

The singular success in commercial enterprise attained by those foreign Protestant refugees who fled to our shores "for conscience sake" proves that the qualities which drove them into exile stood them in good stead even in practical life. And so the sturdy independence of the Friends and their stubborn adherence to their principles were carried with success into business

life, when England, from an agricultural, became a manufacturing country. Such names as those of Bright, Forster, Fry, Gurney, Pease, and other Quaker families remind us how prominent a part, in proportion to their numbers, the Friends have played, not only in modern commerce, but in the Legislature.

The strenuous belief of Friends in the mission of the evangelist led them to seek converts even abroad. Many of our ancestors and their wives became public ministers of the Society of Friends, and Iceland and North America were visited by William (p. 15), (the son of the martyred James), who died in the middle of the last century, and Mauritius, Cape Colony, and Van Dieman's Land by James Backhouse (p. 37), of York, 1831-41, as missionaries.

William Backhouse (p. 15), the first missionary, and the last yeoman of his line, left Yealand, the home of his ancestors, removed to Over Kellett about 1727, becoming, as he tells us in his will, a "dealer in yarn;" and there he died. His son James (p. 17) was the first settler in Darlington, where, together with his sons, he carried on the business of flax dresser and linen manufacturer, and established in 1774 the banking house, now a household word in the north of England.

From this date the various members of the family have interested themselves in the principal commercial enterprises in the palatinate. Conspicuous among them may be named Jonathan Backhouse (p. 25), of Darlington, silver medallist of the Society of Arts, who was a promoter of the Stockton and Darlington Railway—the first to carry passengers—and who yet, amongst his varied engagements, found time, as did his wife, to travel extensively as ministers of the Society of Friends. Another, Thomas Backhouse (p. 34), of York, was a prominent director both of railways and of banks; while his younger brother James (p. 37), one of the missionaries referred to, now represented by his grandson and namesake, was a well-known York botanist. This recital may fittingly close with a reference to the late Edward Backhouse (p. 32), author of "Early Church History," so well known in Sunderland (see "Dictionary of National Biography"), and to the present head of the family and of the bank, Edmund Backhouse (p. 11), who was Darlington's first Member of Parliament, 1868-74, and 1874-80.

Nor does this exhaust the roll, for among collaterals is John Wakefield (p. 64), of Kendal, founder of another and equally well-known banking house, Wakefields, Crewdsons and Co.; and a casual glance at the names in the index will doubtless recall other triumphs in commerce by many offshoots of the family.

The 130 portraits which illustrate this work will lend a hitherto unique charm to the book, and their appearance in a work of this kind is due in the first instance to the acquiescence of T. W. Backhouse (p. 33), of West Hendon House. To W. Ecroyd (p. 36), of Lomeshaye, Nelson (editor of "Court Rolls of the Honor of Clitheroe," 2 vols.), the family is also indebted for contributing much original matter, for revising proofs, and for the pedigrees in the wills' volume, which has expanded far beyond its intended limits, and which cannot fail to be correspondingly appreciated by the genealogical faculty, though the wills are tantalizing to us in their refusal to illustrate the history of this family to any appreciable extent. My hope is, however, that our combined efforts will be approved by our kin, and be a fresh encouragement to me in my life-long exertions against spurious titles, spurious genealogy, and spurious coat armour.

It is not a little singular that in the United States, where families are now widely scattered and more difficult to trace than with us, there is infinitely more of the family feeling, as exhibited in numerous family histories and interesting family gatherings. One may fairly hope that such works as this tend to foster here also a wholesome family spirit, an intelligent and rational interest in our forefathers. To quote from a well-known writer who has not long passed away: "We shall surely not be the less at home in our own generation if we bear in mind that we are the heirs and scholars of the generations that went before us, if we now and then stop in our own course to thank the memory of those without whom our own course could not have been run, if we are ready at every fitting moment to praise 'famous men and our fathers that begat us.'"

JOSEPH FOSTER.

21, BOUNDARY ROAD, LONDON, N.W.,
March, 1894.

Backhouse, of Darlington.

JOHN BACKHOUSE, of Moss-side near Yealand Redman, co. Lanc., yeoman, died in 1690. See page 13. = SARAH, daughter of William Jackson, of Yealand Redmayne, by his wife Mabel, heiress of her brother John Carr, of Ridgend, in Mansergh, born about 1626, died 1706.

A. HANNAH BACKHOUSE, born 1658, died 1729. = JOHN CUMMING, of Hilderstone, mar. 1682, died in 1697. See page 48.

THOMAS BACKHOUSE, of Yealand Redman, born 1661, died 1729. = ALICE, daughter of Richard Becke, of Wythmore in Westmorland, mar. 1696, died 1700. See page 13.

SARAH BACKHOUSE, born 1664, mar. 1688, died 1697, 1st wife. = GEORGE ROBINSON, of Yealand Conyers, died 1719. See page 14.

JAMES BACKHOUSE, of Yealand Conyers, born 1668, died in Lancaster Castle, 1697 (1st husband). See page 14. = JANET, daughter of John Godsalve, of Yealand Conyers, mar. 1691. = JOHN ROBINSON, of Yealand, mar. 1701, 2nd husband.

NATHAN HUBBERSTIE = MARY, daughter of Thomas Thornton, of Caton, co. Lanc. (J. B.'s 1st wife), mar. 1715, died 1716. = JOHN BACKHOUSE, of Hornby, born 1693, died 1739. See page 14. = MARGARET (2nd wife), daughter of John and Ruth Ayrey, of Kendal, born about 1694, mar. 1720, died 1772. See page 14.

WILLIAM BACKHOUSE, of Yealand, a minister of the Society of Friends, born 1696, died 1761. See page 15. = AGNES, daughter of Richard Atkinson, of Monk Coniston, born in 1697, mar. in 1720, died in 1773.

JAMES BACKHOUSE, of West Lodge, Darlington, flax-dresser and linen manufacturer, established the bank at Darlington 1774, born 1721, died 1798. See page 17. = JANE, only child of Jonathan Hedley, of Darlington, born 1718, mar. at Stockton 1746, died in 1805.

WILLIAM BACKHOUSE, born 1724, sometime of New York, died there 1792, mar. ELIZABETH, daughter of Jonathan Thornton, of Caton. She died 1750. See page 16.

B. AGNES BACKHOUSE, born 1730, mar. 1764, died 1797. = JOHN HARRISON, of Darlington, born 1725, died 1800. See page 39.

JOHN BACKHOUSE, of Lancaster, born 1733, died in New York 1775, mar. 1757 JANE, daughter of George Dodgson, of Kendal. She died 1763. See page 16.

JONATHAN BACKHOUSE, of Darlington, banker, born 1747, mar. 1774, died 1826. See page 17. = ANN, 2nd daughter of Edward Pease, of Darlington, born 1746, died there in 1826.

C. JAMES BACKHOUSE, of Darlington, banker, born 1757, mar. 1787, died 1804. See page 34. = MARY, daughter of Nathan Dearman, of Thorne, Yorks, born 1764, died 24th May, 1838.

D. ELIZABETH BACKHOUSE, born 1777, mar. 1799, died 1843. = THOMAS RICHARDSON, of Sunderland, died 1835. See pages 17, 18.

JONATHAN BACKHOUSE, of Darlington, banker, born 1779, mar. 1811, died 1842. See page 25. = HANNAH CHAPMAN, elder daughter and co-heir of Joseph Gurney, of Norwich, died 1850.

E. WILLIAM BACKHOUSE, of Darlington, banker, born 1779, died 1844, mar. 1806, MARY, daughter of John Dixon, of Cockfield. She died 1874. See page 27.

F. EDWARD BACKHOUSE, of Sunderland, banker, born 1781, died 1860, mar. 1807, MARY, daughter of Edward Robson. She died 1860. See page 31.

JOHN BACKHOUSE, of Darlington, banker, married twice, and died 17th Aug., 1847. See page 22.

JANE BACKHOUSE, born 1787, mar. 1815, died 1873. = EDWARD ROBSON, of Darlington, died 1819.

ANN BACKHOUSE ROBSON, mar. 1st to HENRY WHITWELL, and 2nd to DAVID DALE. See pages, 22, 23.

G. JANE GURNEY BACKHOUSE, born 1814, mar. 1844, died 1860. = ROBERT BARCLAY FOX, of Falmouth, died 1855. See page 25.

H. ANNE BACKHOUSE, born 1815, mar. 1843, died 1845. = JOHN HODGKIN, of Lewes, died in 1875. See page 26.

EDMUND BACKHOUSE, of Darlington, banker and M.P. 1868-80, born 1824. See next page. = JULIET MARY, elder daughter and eventually sole heir of Charles Fox, of Trebah, Cornwall, mar. 1848.

JONATHAN EDMUND BACKHOUSE, of Darlington, banker, born 1849. = FLORENCE, daughter of Sir John Salusbury-Trelawny, Bart., mar. 1871.

SARAH JULIET, died 1880, mar. 1876, to HORATIO N. PYM, of London.

CHARLES HUBERT BACKHOUSE, of Darlington, banker, born 1856. = MAUDE CONSTANCE, daughter of H. Ritchie, Esq., of Ceylon, mar. 1880.

MILLICENT EVELYN BACKHOUSE, born 1862.

EDMUND TRELAWNY BACKHOUSE, born 1873. OLIVER, born 1876. ROGER and MILES, born 1878. HARRIET JANE, born 1880.

JULIET MAUDE, born 1881. HUBERT EDMUND, born 1883. CHARLES LLEWELLYN, born 1884.

JONATHAN BACKHOUSE,
Of Darlington, 1779-1842.
See Page 25.

HANNAH C. BACKHOUSE,
1787-1850.
See Page 25.

JONATHAN BACKHOUSE,
Of Darlington, 1747-1826
See Page 17.

EDMUND BACKHOUSE,
Of Darlington.

MRS BACKHOUSE.

BACKHOUSE OF DARLINGTON.

EDMUND BACKHOUSE, of Darlington, banker, J.P. co. Durham, and for Yorkshire (N.R.), M.P. Darlington, 1868-80 (youngest son of Jonathan Backhouse, of Darlington, see page 26), born 28th Nov. 1824; married 22nd Sept., 1848, Juliet Mary, elder daughter and eventually sole heir of Charles Fox, of Trebah, Cornwall, and has had 3 sons and 2 daughters:

(1) Jonathan Edmund Backhouse, of the Rookery, Middleton Tyas, Richmond, Yorks, J.P. (North Riding), born 15th Nov., 1849; married 29th Nov., 1871, Florence, daughter of Sir John Salusbury-Trelawny, Bart., of Trelawny, Cornwall, and has had 5 sons and a daughter:

- (1) Edmund Trelawny Backhouse, postmaster of Merton College, Oxford, 1892, from Winchester College, born 20th Oct., 1873.
- (2) Roland Charles Backhouse, born 15th Dec., 1874, died 18th Dec., 1877.
- (3) Oliver Backhouse, R.N., born 5th June, 1876.
- (4) Roger Roland Charles Backhouse, R.N., born 24th Nov., 1878, twin with
- (5) Miles Roland Charles Backhouse.
- (6) Harriet Jane Backhouse, born 12th March, 1880.

(2) Charles Fox Backhouse, died 24th Aug., 1851, aged 2 months.

(3) Sarah Juliet Backhouse, born 6th Dec., 1852, died 18th Jan., 1880, having married 12th Sept., 1876, as 1st wife to Horatio Noble Pym, of London, Solicitor (son of Rev. William Wollaston Pym, rector of Willian, Herts), his 2nd wife being Jane Hannah Backhouse Fox (see page 26).

(4) Charles Hubert Backhouse, of Ainderby Hall, Yorks, born 22nd Sept., 1856; married 25th Nov., 1880, Maude Constance (born 4th Feb., 1855), daughter of H. Ritchie, Esq., of Ceylon, and has 2 sons and 2 daughters:

- (1) Juliet Maude Backhouse, born 18th Oct., 1881.
- (2) Hubert Edmund Backhouse, born 4th Jan., 1883.
- (3) Charles Llewellyn Backhouse, born 2nd April, 1884.
- (4) Indiana Richeuda Backhouse, born 10th July, 1886.

(5) Millicent Evelyn Backhouse, born 22nd Oct., 1862.

BACKHOUSE,

FORMERLY OF YEALAND REDMAN, CO. LANC.

Lineage.

ROBERT BACKUS, of Yealand, parish of Warton, bond to administer his goods given by Thomas Astley and another, *circa* 1604 (see page 75), probably father of Jane Backhouse, baptized at Warton 27th Feb., 1593.

RICHARD BACKHOUSE, of Yealand Redmayne, parish of Warton. Inventory of his goods taken 16th Sept., 1640, by Richard Bacchus and others (see page 75). Richard Backhouse, of Yelland, and others, were plaintiffs, *versus* Edward Holt and others, concerning lands in Yealand, Warton, Coniarse, Over Kellet, &c., and a demesne called Duorslacke, in occupation of Thomas Middleton, of Leighton (see *Exchequer depositions, Lancashire*, 12th Feb., 3 Chas. I., 1627); perhaps baptized at Warton 13th August, 1583; buried there 13th Sept., 1640, was probably father of a daughter; Jane Backhouse, who was a legatee, 1641, under the will of John Backhouse, of Warton (see pp. 75, 76), "to Jane Bachus, the late daughter of Richard Bachus, late of Yealand Redman, deceased, one lamb"; baptized 11th April, 1626.

RICHARD BACKHOUSE, of Yelland Conyers, co. Lanc. Inventory of his goods taken 6th May, 1666. Bond dated 6th June, 1667, signed by Anne Backhouse, of Yealand Conyers, and the mark of Robert Backhouse (see page 76).

---

(1) JOHN BACKHOUSE, of whom presently, was probably nearly related to and even brother of

(2) Richard Backhouse, of Yelland, parish of Warton, to whom his wife Mary and his son Robert administered 23rd Dec., 1696 (see page 77). He had a son and probably 2 daughters:

(1) Robert Backhouse, living 1696; made his will 1st Aug., 1728, in which he named his nephew, Robert Backhouse, and "the eight children" of his niece Hannah, wife of Joseph Bispham (see page 79).

(2) Ann Backhouse, buried at Hilderstone, co. Lanc., 1676, xi. 2; married at William Waithman's house, Lindeth, 1672, iii. 19, as 2nd wife to Robert Hubberstie, of Yealand, who died 1706, viii. 12, having had by her 2 sons and daughter:

(1) Nathan Hubberstie, of Yelland, husbandman, born 1673, vii. 6, died 1709, iii. 15; married 1697, vi. 17 at her father's house, Mary, daughter of Thomas Thornton, of Deepclough in Littledale. She died 1716, v. 23, having re-married 1715, iv. 2, to John, elder son of James Backhouse, of Yealand Conyers (see page 14).

(2) Hannah Hubberstie, born at Yealand 1675, iv. 8, died 1763, vi. 1, aged 88; married at Yealand 1699/1700, i. 6, to Joseph Bispham, son of John, of Bickersteth, co. Lanc., and Mary Bastwell his wife. He died 1750, iii. 3, having had 9 children, of whom (see page 74) the eldest surviving son:

BENJAMIN BISPHAM, married at Yelland Conyers 1727, v. 5, Sarah, daughter of Thomas Backhouse, of Yealand Redman, co. Lanc. (see pages 13, 14), and had issue (see page 74).

(3) Isaac Hubberstie, born 1676, x. 28, buried at Hilderstone 14th proximo.

(3) Alice Backhouse, died a widow at Over Kellet 1727, ix. 1; married at Yelland 1676, iv. 4, to William Hugginson, of Yelland, who died 1707, viii. 1 or 19.

JONATHAN E. BACKHOUSE
See Page 11.

MRS. J. E. BACKHOUSE

EDMUND T. BACKHOUSE.

CHARLES H. BACKHOUSE
See Page 11.

MRS. CHARLES H. BACKHOUSE

JOHN BACKHOUSE,[1] of Moss Side, near Yealand Redman, co. Lanc., yeoman, joined the Society of Friends at an early period in its history, for according to Besse's "Sufferings of Friends" he and other friends were taken from their meeting for worship at Yealand in 1st month (March), 1660—confined in Lancaster Castle until the summer of 1661, and set at liberty without examination, and for refusing to pay tithes his cattle were sold in 1684 (see Besse's "Sufferings," i. pp. 307, 488, 489, etc.); married, about 1650, Sarah, only daughter of William Jackson, of Yealand Redmayne (by his wife, Mabel Carr,[2] heir of her brother, John Carr, of Ridgend in Mansergh); he died at Yealand, and was buried at Hilderstone, near Yealand, 1690, iii. 9. Made his will 10 April, 1690, proved 29 May following, inventory dated 14th same month (see page 77). His wife Sarah adopted Friends' principles when 27 years of age, through the preaching of Geo. Fox himself in 1653, and became a public minister of that society ("Piety Promoted," vol. i.); she died 1706, v. 30, having had 4 sons and 2 daughters, all born at Yealand Redman :

(1) John Backhouse, born 1656, vi. 16, died 1657, iii. 30, buried 31st.

(2) James Backhouse, died at Yealand 1657, iii. 29.

(3) Hannah Backhouse, born 1658, viii. 28, died at Hilderstone 1729, iv. 8; married at Richard Lancaster's house, Yelland, 1682, iii. 24, to John, son of Edward Cumming, of Hilderstone, where he died 1697, xi. 28, having had 2 sons and 3 daughters (see page 48).

(4) Thomas Backhouse, of Yealand Redman, co. Lanc., yeoman, born there 1661, vii. 17, and died 1729, iii. 22; made his will 20th May, 1729, proved 1st October following (see pages 78, 79); married at Lambrigge 1696, ix. 16, Alice, daughter of Richard Becke, of Wythmore, in Westmorland, she was born 1671, vi. 8, and buried 1700, iv. 11, having had a son and daughter :

> **(1)** John Backhouse (1729), of Hilderstone, yeoman, born 1698, v. 26; died 4th May, 1779, aged 80, buried at Yealland; made his will 26th Dec., 1763, proved 19th June, 1779 (see page 81); devised all his property to his cousin, John Cumming, whose daughter Hannah conveyed Hilderstone by marriage to the father of the present owner (see page 16).
>
> **(2)** Sarah Backhouse (1729), born at Beckhouses in Grayrigg 1700, iv. 29; buried 1731.

[1] John Backhouse, yeoman, of Yealand Redmayne, by indenture dated 20 July, 18 Chas. II., 1666, purchased from Christopher Robinson, of Yealand Redmayne, a close of land called Thrygill end close, containing $3\frac{1}{3}$ roods, and also a parcel containing $\frac{1}{2}$ rood, rent 1/.

John Backhouse, of Yealand Redmayne, co. Lanc., one of the customary tenants of the manor of Yelland, was admitted tenant of $4\frac{1}{2}$ acres of land in Yelland Redmayne, of his own purchase from Thos. Mason, of Warton. Yearly rent 5/8. Fine 45/4 at a court held 13 April, 1669.

John Backhouse appeared among the tenants of Yelland Redmayne at a Court Baron for the manor of Yelland, held at Yelland Storrs, 20 June, 34 Chas. II., 1682.

[2] Mabel Jackson, John Backhouse, and William Hugginson, of Yealand, in the parish of Warton, by deed dated 20 Feb., 1663, were bound to the Rev. Joseph Cradock in the sum of £100 to perform the last will of John Carr, brother of the said Mabel Jackson, whose only daughter Sarah was wife of the said John Backhouse.

vii. 20 (or viii. 29); married at Yelland Conyers 1727, v. 5, to Benjamin, son of Joseph, of Yelland Conyers (see page 12), and had at least 3 sons and a daughter (see page 74).

(5) Sarah Backhouse, born 1664, xi. 4, died 1697, iv. 9; married at Richard Lancaster's house at Yelland 1688, xi. 4, as 1st wife to George (son of George) Robinson, of Yealand Conyers, who died 1719, viii. (or ix.) 6, having had 3 sons and a daughter:

(1) Sarah Robinson, born 1691, vi. 3 or 13, probably died 1723, ii. 25.

(2) George Robinson, of Yelland Conyers, co. Lanc., born 1693, v. 30, probably died 1756, xii. 1, then of Cathouse (? Colthouse); married 1st at Lancaster 172¾, i. 11, Elizabeth, daughter of John Yeats, of Lancaster, schoolmaster; she died 1727, ii. 24. He married 2ndly at Swarthmore 1731, iii. 11, Agnes Hest, of Ulverston, milliner.

(3) Thomas Robinson, born 169⅚, i. 6, died 1696, ii. 25.

(4) John Robinson, died 1697, vi. 9.

(6) JAMES BACKHOUSE, next mentioned.

JAMES BACKHOUSE, of Yealand Conyers, yeoman, born there 1668, xi. 24; committed to Lancaster Castle at the suit of the Dean and Chapter of Worcester, on a plea "*de excommunicatione capiendae*," for refusal to pay tithes, and to "answer his libel" on oath in the Bishop's Court, and died "a prisoner" in the Castle 1697, iv. 13, aged 29 (see "Piety Promoted," vol. i.); his will dated 3rd May, 1697 (see page 78). He married at Yealand Conyers (in Robert Hubbersty's house) 1691, xi. 14, Janet, daughter of John Godsalve, of Yealand Conyers (she re-married 1701, vii. 10, to John Robinson, of Yealand), and had 2 sons and a daughter, all born at Yealand:

(1) John Backhouse, of Hornby, co. Lanc., yeoman, born 169⅔, xii. 27, died at Hornby 1739, xii. 6, buried at Yelland; made his will 19th Nov., 1739, proved 15th Dec., 1740 (see page 80); married 1st, 1715, iv. 2, Mary, widow of Nathan Hubberstie, and daughter of Thomas Thornton of Caton, co. Lanc.; she died 1716, v. 23, leaving a daughter, (1) Elizabeth, born 1716, v. 11, who died, 1720, xi. 21. He (J. B.) married 2ndly at Shapp, 1720, i. 2, Margaret, daughter of Ruth Ayrey, of Kendal (widow of John "Arey," of Shapp); she died 11th July, 1772, aged 78, having had 2 sons and 3 daughters:

(2) Mary Backhouse, born 1722, viii. 20; married at Yealand Conyers 1741, ix. 8, to James Metcalfe, of Bainbridge, Yorks, mercer (son of Alexander, of Marset, Yorks); he was born 1716, i. x., and had 5 sons:

(1) John Metcalfe, of Gray's Inn, porter.

(2) Alexander Metcalfe, of Countriside in Wensleydale, cordwainer.

(3) James Metcalfe, of Westhouse, in parish of Thornton-in-Craven, collier, married Ellen.

(4) Thomas Metcalfe, of Fleet Street, Bethnal Green, cotton manufacturer.

(5) Francis Metcalfe, of Preston, chaise driver.

JOHN MOUNSEY
See Page 31.

MRS JOHN MOUNSEY.

LUCY E. MOUNSEY

EDWARD B. MOUNSEY
See Page 31.

MRS EDWARD B. MOUNSEY

(3) James Ayrey Backhouse, born 1725, ix. 10, died young.
(4) Ruth Backhouse, born 1727, xii. 26, died 1733, ii. 17.
(5) John Backhouse, born 1729, i. 25, drowned 1753, vi. 2, in Windermere, in going to Yealand meeting.
(6) Margaret Backhouse, born 1731, xi. 12, died 29th November, 1817, aged 86, then of Kirkland, Westmorland; married to her cousin, John Braithwaite, of Mislet, yeoman,[1] (only son of Richard, of Mislet in Windermere, and his wife Mary, youngest daughter of John Airey, of Shap); he was born 1730, iii. 20, and died 11th March, 1792, aged 62, having had 4 sons and 2 daughters:

(1) John Airey Braithwaite, of Lancaster, surgeon, the propounder of the once well-known medical preparation, "the black drop," died *s.p.* in Lancaster, 12th March, 1810, aged 57; married at Bishop Auckland, 20th June, 1796, Sarah, only child of Samuel Bewley, of Coundon, co. Durham (by his wife Frances Dodshon, grand-daughter of Thomas Forster, of Hawthorne, co. Durham); she died 24th May, 1830.
(2) Richard Braithwaite, of Kendal, ironmonger, married Emma Copeland, and had an only daughter:
(1) Emma Braithwaite, born 28th Dec., 1784; married thrice: 1st to —— Harrison, of Kirby Stephen, and lastly to —— Broster.
(3) Mary Braithwaite, married to Richard Cookson, of Kendal.
(4) Margaret Braithwaite, of Mislet, died 16th Feb., 1825, aged 59.
(5) James Braithwaite, of Kirkland, died 14th Sept., 1806, aged 37.
(6) Thomas Braithwaite, of Kirkland in Westmorland, died 18th Feb., 1822, aged 49, married Jane Bindloss, and had a daughter Hannah, of Kendal.

(2) Sarah Backhouse, born 1694, v. 6, died 1699, vi. 30.
(3) WILLIAM BACKHOUSE, next mentioned.

WILLIAM BACKHOUSE, of Yealand, yeoman (1720), removed to Over Kellet about 1727, became a dealer in yarn, "40 years" a minister of the Society of Friends, and in that capacity visited Iceland and North America (see "Piety Promoted," vol. ii.); born at Yealand, 169⅚, i. 13, died at Kellet 1761, v. 21; made his will 6th March, 1761, proved 6th June following (see page 80); married at Colthouse 1720, iv. 21, Agnes, grand-daughter of Richard Atkinson, of Monk Coniston, and dau. of William Atkinson, of Low Wray, near Hawkshead (by his wife Sarah, daughter of Reginald Walker, of Fell Foot, Little Langdale); she was born 1697, xii. 4, and died 28th Nov., 1773, buried 1st Dec., having had 6 sons and 7 daughters:
(1) JAMES BACKHOUSE, of whom see page 17.
(2) William Backhouse, sometime of New York, born at Yealand 1724, iii. 24, died in

[1] Another pedigree erroneously styles him Thomas Braithwaite, of Kendal, son of Richard, of Mislet.

New York, 25th August, 1792; married at Whitby 1749, x. 5, Elizabeth, daughter of Jonathan Thornton, of Caton, co. Lanc. (by his wife Margaret Birket); she died there 1750, vii. 23, leaving a son:

THOMAS BACKHOUSE, of West Lodge, Darlington, sometime chairman of Lloyd's, born at Lancaster 1750, vii. 14, died at Seaton Carew 5th Oct., 1824; married 11th Sept., 1792, Sarah, daughter of John and Susannah Goad, of London, she died at Forest Hill 26th March, 1805, aged 35, having had 2 sons:

(1) John Goad Backhouse, born 10th July, 1793, died 5th Aug. following.

(2) William Backhouse, born 14th Sept., 1794, died 2nd Oct. following.

(3) Sarah Backhouse, born at Yealand 1726, vi. 31, died unmarried at Kellet 1766, xi. 1.

(4) Jane Backhouse, born at Kellet 1728, vii. 1, died at Kendal 1742, xii. —.

(5) Agnes Backhouse, born at Kellet 1730, viii. 14, died 25th March, 1797; married at Darlington 1764, ix. 13, to John Harrison, of Darlington (son of Richard and Mary Harrison, of Burton, near Barnsley); he was born 1725, iv. 20, and died at Darlington 29th Jan., 1800, having had, a son, and 2 daughters (see page 39).

(6) John Backhouse, of Lancaster, merchant, born at Kellet 1733, i. 30, died in New York 31st Jan., 1775; he married at Kellet 1757, i. 3, Jane, daughter of George and Elizabeth Dodgson, of Kendal; she died at Lancaster 1763, i. 5; administration at Lancaster 18th Feb. following (see page 81); having had 2 sons:

(1) William Backhouse, born 1758, ii. 13, buried 1763, ii. 28.

(2) George Backhouse, of Kendal, ironmonger and stamp distributor, born 1760, iii. 9, died 23rd October, 1830; married at Yealand 4th January, 1804, to his 3rd cousin, Hannah, daughter of John Cumming, of Hilderstone, parish of Warton, co. Lanc., and eventually sole heir of her brother Edward (see page 48); she died at Kendal 18th Sept., 1842, aged 74, having had a son and daughter:

(1) Hannah Backhouse, born 16th Feb., 1805, died unmarried, at Hilderstone, 15th Nov., 1865, aged 60.

(2) John Backhouse, of Hilderstone, born 21st Jan., 1808, died there 15th April, 1879; buried in Burton church; married at Warton 11th May, 1854, Mary, daughter of William Titterington, of Yealand Redmayne, and had a son and 4 daughters:

(1) Edward Cumming Backhouse, of Hilderstone, born at Burton in Kendal, 29th Aug., 1855; married there, 23rd Nov., 1882, Harriet, daughter of William Stagg, of Manor House, Burton; she died 5 December, 1883, having had a daughter:

(1) Hilda Cumming Backhouse, born 25th Nov., 1883.

(2) Mary Ann Backhouse, born at Priest Hutton, 31st Aug., 1858; married 8th March, 1883, to Thomas Rauthmell, of Brooke House, Holme, Westmorland, and has a son and 3 daughters:

EDWARD MOUNSEY
See Page 33.

EMILY MOUNSEY
First wife, died 1869

THOMAS E. MOUNSEY

ADA M. MOUNSEY

ELIZABETH L. MOUNSEY

(1) Ethel Mary Rauthmell, born 28th Feb., 1884.
(2) John Rauthmell.
(3) Margaret Isabelle Rauthmell.
(4) Edith Maud Rauthmell.

(3) Susannah Backhouse, born at Priest Hutton 11th Dec., 1860; married 21 Dec., 1886, to Charles Hawkins Copley Woodhead, L.R.C.P., L.R.C.S. Edinb., of Gordon Bank, Luddenden Foot, and has a daughter:

Doris Agatha Backhouse Woodhead, born 6th Nov., 1887.

(4) Louisa Jane Backhouse, born at Priest Hutton 27th Dec., 1864, died at Hilderstone 26th May, 1882, buried in Burton church.

(5) Adelaide Katura Teresa Backhouse, born at Hilderstone 7th Feb., 1867, died at Blackpool 5th May, 1891; married 21st March, 1885, to Richard Vivian Grattan, and had 3 children, who died in infancy.

(7) Thomas Backhouse, of Darlington, born 1736, vi. 1 (or iii. 21), died unmarried at Darlington, 1st Sept., 1792.

(8) James and (9) John, both died young.

(10) Dorothy Backhouse, of Lancaster, born at Kellet 1740 x. $\frac{0}{10}$, died at Lancaster 27th Nov. 1829.

(11) Mary, (12) Margaret, and (13) Ruth, all died young.

JAMES BACKHOUSE, of West Lodge, Darlington, flax dresser and linen manufacturer, and, in conjunction with his sons, established the bank at Darlington in 1774 (eldest son of William, see page 15); born at Yealand 172?, i. 22, died at Darlington 1st April, 1798; married at Stockton 1746, ii. 8, Jane, only child of Jonathan Hedley, of Darlington; she was born there 1718, xii. 27, and died 27th May, 1805, having had 2 sons:

(1) JONATHAN BACKHOUSE, of whom see below.

(2) James Backhouse, of Darlington, banker, born there 1757, vi. 29, died there 18th Dec. 1804; married 8th June, 1787, Mary, daughter of Nathan Dearman, of Thorne, after of Pindar Oaks, Darfield, Yorks; she died at York 24th May, 1838, aged 74, having had 4 sons and 6 daughters (see page 34).

JONATHAN BACKHOUSE, of Darlington, banker, carried on the business of flax dressing and linen manufacture, born at Darlington 1747, x. 13, died at West Lodge, Darlington, 11th Nov., 1826; married 12th May, 1774, Ann, 2nd daughter of Edward Pease, of Darlington (by his wife Elizabeth Coates); she was born 1746, ii. 25, and died 3rd Jan., 1826, having had 6 sons and 4 daughters, all born at Darlington:

(1) William Backhouse, born 15th Feb., 1775, died 19th Jan., 1779.

(2) Jane Backhouse, born at Darlington 27th March, 1776, died 13th March, 1786.

(3) Elizabeth Backhouse, born at Darlington 12th Sept., 1777, and died 2nd March, 1843;

married 17th Oct., 1799, to Thomas Richardson, of Sunderland (son of Thomas and Frances); he died there 29th Oct., 1835, having had 5 sons and 4 daughters :

(1) Thomas Richardson, of Shotley Bridge, born at Sunderland 25th July, 1800, died at Shotley Bridge 2nd April, 1872.

(2) Frances Richardson, died 1801, a twin with

(3) Ann Richardson, born at Sunderland 28th Nov., 1801, died 14th Dec. following.

(4) Jonathan Richardson, managing director of the Northumberland and Durham District Bank, founder of the Derwent, now the Consett, Iron Company, born 16th Nov., 1802; married 12th July, 1827, Ann, daughter of Edward Robson, of Darlington, and died at Woodlands 25th Dec., 1871, having had 2 sons and 4 daughters :

(1) Jonathan Backhouse Richardson, of Shotley Lodge, co. Durham, born 28th April, 1828, died 29th May, 1892; married 16th May, 1850, Rachel, daughter of John Robinson Waite, Esq., of Stoke Newington (by Sarah Pryor, his wife), and had 5 sons and 6 daughters :

(1) Jonathan Richardson, born 17th May, 1851; married June, 1873, Elizabeth, daughter of H. —— Grainger, Esq., of Westminster.

(2) Charles Richardson, born 4th May, 1852; married 9th May, 1881, Mai, eldest daughter of J. W. Shiell, Esq., of Chester-le-Street, co. Durham.

(3) Henry Edward Richardson, born 1st June, 1853.

(4) Edmund Louis Richardson, born 18th Oct., 1854, died 16th April, 1865.

(5) Amelia Florence Richardson, born 11th Oct., 1855; married 26th Jan., 1880, to Edward Harrington Hudson, Esq., who died 1891.

(6) Thomas Walter Richardson, born 10th Feb., 1857.

(7) Marion Richardson, born 10th May, 1858; married 14th Dec., 1891, to Sherlock Vignoles Willis, major, retired, late Royal Scots and Suffolk Regts.

(8) Annie Richardson, born 1859, and died same year.

(9) Isabella Richardson, born 12th Feb., 1861, married 4th Dec., 1893, to Dalrymple James Belgrave, barrister-at-law, Inner Temple, 1876, 2nd son of late Thomas of Kilworth, co. Leicester, Commander R.N.

(10) Amy Erlinda Richardson, born 23rd Oct., 1864.

(11) Anne Richardson, born 2nd April, 1866.

(2) Lucy Ann Richardson, born at Newcastle 24th Dec., 1829; married at Shotley Bridge 28th July, 1852, to Jonathan Priestman, of Derwent Lodge, Shotley Bridge, J.P., sometime a managing director of the Consett Iron Company, born 15th Dec., 1825, and died 21st Dec., 1888, having had 2 sons and 4 daughters, all born at Shotley Bridge :

(1) Frances Priestman, born 24th March, 1854; married at Shotley Bridge, 4th May, 1880, to Joseph Pumphrey, of that place, and has 2 sons and 2 daughters, all born there :

JOHN BACKHOUSE
1784-1847
See Page 22

ELIZA, FIRST WIFE OF JOHN BACKHOUSE

ELIZA BARCLAY
Daughter of John Backhouse
See Page 22

... 20th Jan., 1881.

August,
r. Shiell,

).

ily, 1881.

eb., 1832,
aughter of

N.

4th May,
e Peile, of

JAMES BACK
Darlington,
manufacture
at Darlingto
1758. See

, to Rev.

JONATH
born 17

[19]

).

D
ELIZABETH
HOUSE, born
mar. 1799,
1843.

9, to Rev.
3, Rector

o Stratton

Jo
D
bo

Jo
R
L
1
1

JONATHA
born 185
ELIZA
GRAINGE
CHARL
born 185
MAI SH

Richardson, of Shotley.

JOHN BACKHOUSE, of Moss-side near Yealand Redman, co. Lanc., yeoman, died in 1690. See page 13. = SARAH, daughter of William Jackson, of Yealand Redmayne, by his wife Mabel, heiress of her brother John Carr, of Ridgend, in Mansergh, born about 1626, died 1706.

A. HANNAH BACKHOUSE, born 1658, died 1729. = JOHN CUMMING, of Hilderstone, mar. 1682, died in 1697. See page 48.

THOMAS BACKHOUSE, of Yealand Redman, born 1661, died 1729. = ALICE, daughter of Richard Becke, of Wythmore in Westmorland, mar. 1696, died 1700. See page 13.

SARAH BACKHOUSE, born 1664, mar. 1688, died 1697, 1st wife. = GEORGE ROBINSON, of Yealand Conyers, died 1719. See page 14.

JAMES BACKHOUSE, of Yealand Conyers, born 1668, died in Lancaster Castle, 1697 (1st husband). See page 14. = JANET, daughter of John Godsalve, of Yealand Conyers, mar. 1691. = JOHN ROBINSON, of Yealand, mar. 1701, 2nd husband.

NATHAN HUBBERSTIE = MARY, daughter of Thomas Thornton, of Caton, co. Lanc. (J. B.'s 1st wife), mar. 1715, died 1716. = JOHN BACKHOUSE, of Hornby, born 1693, died 1739. See page 14. = MARGARET (2nd wife), daughter of John and Ruth Ayrey, of Kendal, born about 1694, mar. 1720, died 1772. See page 14.

WILLIAM BACKHOUSE, of Yealand, a minister of the Society of Friends, born 1696, died 1761. See page 15. = AGNES, daughter of Richard Atkinson, of Monk Coniston, born in 1697, mar. in 1720, died in 1773.

JAMES BACKHOUSE, of West Lodge, Darlington, flax-dresser and linen manufacturer, established the bank at Darlington 1774, born 1721, died 1798. See page 17. = JANE, only child of Jonathan Hedley, of Darlington, born 1718, mar. at Stockton 1746, died in 1805.

WILLIAM BACKHOUSE, born 1724, sometime of New York, died there 1792, mar. ELIZABETH, daughter of Jonathan Thornton, of Caton. She died 1750. See page 16.

B. AGNES BACKHOUSE, born 1730, mar. 1764, died 1797. = JOHN HARRISON, of Darlington, born 1725, died 1800. See page 39.

JOHN BACKHOUSE, of Lancaster, born 1733, died in New York 1775, mar. 1757 JANE, daughter of George Dodgson, of Kendal. She died 1763. See page 16.

JONATHAN BACKHOUSE, of Darlington, banker, born 1747, mar. 1774, died 1826. See page 17. = ANN, 2nd daughter of Edward Pease, of Darlington, born 1746, died there in 1826.

C. JAMES BACKHOUSE, of Darlington, banker, born 1757, mar. 1787, died 1804. See page 34. = MARY, daughter of Nathan Dearman, of Thorne, Yorks, born 1764, died 24th May, 1838.

D. ELIZABETH BACKHOUSE, born 1777, mar. 1799, died 1843. = THOMAS RICHARDSON, of Sunderland, died 1835.

JONATHAN BACKHOUSE, of Darlington, banker, born 1779, mar. 1811, died 1842. = HANNAH CHAPMAN, elder daughter and co-heir of Joseph Gurney, of Norwich, died 1850. See page 25.

E. WILLIAM BACKHOUSE, of Darlington, banker, born 1779, died 1844, mar. 1806, MARY, daughter of John Dixon, of Cockfield. She died 1874. See page 27.

F. EDWARD BACKHOUSE, of Sunderland, banker, born 1781, died 1860, mar. 1807, MARY, daughter of Edward Robson. She died 1860. See page 31.

JOHN BACKHOUSE, of Darlington, banker, married twice, and died 17th Aug., 1847. See page 22.

JANE BACKHOUSE, born 1787, mar. 1815, died 1873. = EDWARD ROBSON, of Darlington, died 1819.

ANN BACKHOUSE ROBSON, mar. 1st to HENRY WHITWELL, and 2nd to DAVID DALE. See pages, 22, 23.

JONATHAN RICHARDSON, founder of the Derwent, now the Consett Iron Company, born 1802, died 1871. See page 18. = ANN, daughter of EDWARD ROBSON, of Darlington, mar. 12th July, 1827.

EDWARD RICHARDSON, born 1810, mar. 1843, died 1886. See page 21. = GULIELMA, daughter of SAMUEL TUKE, of York, died 1888.

JONATHAN BACKHOUSE RICHARDSON, of Shotley Lodge, co. Durham, born 1828, mar. 1850, died 1892. See page 18. = RACHEL, dau. of JOHN R. WAITE, of London.

LUCY ANN RICHARDSON, born 1829, mar. 1852. See page 18. = JONATHAN PRIESTMAN, of Shotley Bridge, born 1825, died 1888.

ELIZABETH FRANCES RICHARDSON, born 1835, mar. 1857. See page 20. = GEORGE PEILE, of Greenwood, Shotley Bridge.

AMELIA RICHARDSON, born 1837, mar. 1859. See page 20. = REV. ROBERT GEORGE WILLIS, B.A., Oxon., rector of Goodmanham, Yorks, 1881.

Children of Jonathan Backhouse Richardson: JONATHAN R., born 1851, mar. ELIZABETH GRAINGER. CHARLES R., born 1852, mar. [illegible]. HENRY E. R., born 1853. AMELIA F. R., mar. 1880, EDW. H. HUDSON, who died 1891. THOMAS W. R., born 1857. MARION R., mar. 1891 to MAJOR WILLIS. ISABELLA R., born 1861. AMY E. R., born 1864. ANNE R., born 1866.

Children of Lucy Ann and Jonathan Priestman: FRANCES P., mar. 1880, JOSEPH PUMPHREY, of Shotley Bridge. See page 18. FRANCIS P., born 1855, mar. 1883, CECILIA M., daughter of DR. SHIELL. See page 20. LUCY, born 1859. LEWIS, born 1863. KATHARINE, born 1872.

Children of Elizabeth Frances and George Peile: MARY P., born 1859, mar. 1892, to REV. A. G. BRAUND. HELEN, born 1860. FRANCES, born 1861. GEO. HENRY, born 1862. EVALEEN, born 1874, dead.

Children of Amelia and Rev. Robert George Willis: MARY W., mar. 1880, to STRATTON C. KNOTT, and has three children. ANN, born 1861. AMELIA, born 1863. ROBERT, born 1864. FRANCES, born 1865. EVELYN, born 1867. WILLIAM, born 1869. ALICE M., b. 1870. THOMAS R., born 1873. HELEN, born 1874. EDWARD, born 1876. AGNES M., born 1876. REGINALD, born 1879. NONA RUTH, b. 1881.

(1) Charles Ernest Pumphrey, born 29th Jan., 1881.
(2) Lettice Margaret Pumphrey, born 14th Nov., 1884.
(3) Dorothy Frances Pumphrey, born 21st Oct., 1888.
(4) John Laurence Pumphrey, born 27th April, 1891.

(2) Francis Priestman, of Derwent Hill, Ebchester, J.P., born 25th August, 1855; married 29th August, 1883, Cecilia Marguerite, daughter of Dr. Shiell, of Chester-le-Street, and has had 2 sons and a daughter:

(1) Faith Hadwen Priestman, born 8th July, 1886.
(2) Francis Noel Priestman, born 9th and died 12th Jan., 1890.
(3) Jonathan Lee Priestman, born 30th Jan., 1892.

(3) Rachel Elizabeth Priestman, born 25th Jan., 1857, died 19th July, 1881.
(4) Lucy Priestman, born 6th March, 1859.
(5) Lewis Priestman, born 22nd Dec., 1863.
(6) Katharine Priestman, born 4th July, 1872.

(3) Thomas Richardson, of the Briary, Shotley Bridge, born 6th Feb., 1832, died *s.p.* 8th Jan., 1877; married 3rd Jan., 1861, Catherine Marion, daughter of John Renton, M.D., of Shotley Bridge.

(4) Elizabeth Frances Richardson, born 21st Jan., 1835; married 14th May, 1857, to George Peile, of Greenwood, Shotley Bridge (son of George Peile, of Whitehaven), and has had 2 sons and 4 daughters:

(1) George Peile, born 27th Feb., and died 15th March, 1858.
(2) Mary Peile, born 15th Feb., 1859; married 12th Jan., 1892, to Rev. Arthur George Braund, M.A. from Downing Coll., Camb., 1889.
(3) Helen Peile, born 2nd Feb., 1860.
(4) Frances Peile, born 12th Aug., 1861.
(5) Henry Peile, born 18th July, 1862.
(6) Evelyn Peile, born 29th Aug., 1864, and died 20th Feb., 1880.

(5) Amelia Richardson, born 24th Feb., 1837; married 15th July, 1859, to Rev. Robert George Willis, B.A. from Magdalen College, Oxford, 1853, Rector of Goodmanham, Yorks, 1881, and has 5 sons and 9 daughters:

(1) Mary Willis, born 5th June, 1860; married 1st July, 1880, to Stratton Collings Knott, Esq., and has 2 sons and a daughter:

(1) Stratton Clark Knott, born 14th April, 1881.
(2) Frances Mary Knott, born 17th March, 1884.
(3) Ellis Anthony Fermor Knott, born 7th Jan., 1886.

(2) Ann Willis, born 14th Sept., 1861.
(3) Amelia Willis, born 13th Feb., 1863.
(4) Robert Willis, born 5th July, 1864.
(5) Frances Willis, born 30th Sept., 1865.

Edward Richardson

Mrs. Edward Richardson

Mrs C A Fox

Thomas E. Richardson

Samuel T Richardson

(6) Evelyn Willis, born 12th Oct., 1867.
(7) William Willis, born 31st Oct., 1869.
(8) Alice Marion Willis, born 26th Dec., 1870.
(9) Thomas Richardson Willis, born 3rd March, 1873.
(10) Helen Willis, born 10th Sept., 1874.
(11) Edward Willis (twin with Agnes Maude), born 28th Dec., 1876.
(12) Agnes Maude (twin with Edward), born 28th Dec., 1876.
(13) Reginald Willis, born 10th May, 1879.
(14) Nona Ruth Willis, born 4th June, 1881.

(6) Priscilla Hunter Richardson, born at Newcastle-upon-Tyne 23rd Jan., 1842, died 25th April, 1843.

(5) James Richardson, born at Sunderland 27th April, 1805, died 31st March, 1807.

(6) Sarah Richardson, born 5th July, 1807, died 13th May, 1870.

(7) Edward Richardson, of Hendon, Torquay, born at Sunderland 26th Feb., 1810, died at Torquay 7th June, 1886; married at York 12th Dec., 1843, Gulielma, daughter of Samuel Tuke, of York; she died at Plymouth 1st Feb., 1888, having had 4 sons and 3 daughters:

(1) Thomas Edward Richardson, Secretary H.M. Prisons Department, New Zealand, born at Sunderland 6th Oct., 1844.

(2) Samuel Tuke Richardson, born at Sunderland 10th July, 1846; married at York 1st May, 1890, Eleanor Wilson, daughter of Henry Ponsonby, of Birkenhead.

(3) Gulielma Maria Richardson, born at Sunderland 28th Feb., 1848; married at Torquay 3rd Sept., 1874, to Charles Alfred Fox, of Widey Court, Plymouth, and has had 4 sons and 4 daughters:

(1) Alice Gulielma Fox, born 9th Oct., 1875, died 20th Aug., 1876.
(2) Charles Reginald Fox, born 16th Aug., 1877.
(3) Gerald Edward Fox, born 4th Nov., 1878, died 30th March, 1879.
(4) Violet Marion Fox, born 19th March, 1880.
(5) Maude Geraldine Fox, born 9th March, 1882.
(6) Harold Richardson Fox, born 27th May, 1884.
(7) Edward Bonvile Fox, born 16th Jan., 1886.
(8) Ethel Gladys Fox, born 26th Sept., 1888.

(4) Priscilla Hack Richardson, born at Whickham, co. Durham, August, 1850.

(5) Elizabeth Richardson, born at Shotley Bridge April, 1852, died Nov., 1858.

(6) Henry James Richardson, born at Torquay 12th Dec., 1855; married at Exmouth 6th Dec., 1888, Marianne Ramsay Ewart, and has a daughter:

Gulielma Ewart Richardson, born at Taunton 30th Nov., 1890.

(7) Arthur Richardson (Dr.), born at Torquay September, 1857.

(8) William Backhouse Richardson, born at Sunderland 18th Sept., 1811, died 25th March, 1812.

(9) Elizabeth Richardson, born 22nd Jan., 1813, died *s.p.* 3rd March, 1878; married 4th Dec., 1850, as 2nd wife to Edwin Octavius Tregelles, Esq., of Derwent Hill, Shotley Bridge, who was born at Falmouth 19th October, 1806, married firstly in 1832 Jenepher (daughter of Abraham Fisher, of Youghal), and died at Neithrop, Banbury, 16th September, 1886.

(4) JONATHAN BACKHOUSE, of whom see page 25.

(5) William Backhouse, of Darlington, banker, born there 17th Nov., 1779, died 9th June 1844; married 27th March, 1806, Mary, daughter of John Dixon, of Cockfield; she was born there 14th Nov., 1783, and died 22nd March, 1874, aged 90, having had 5 sons and 3 daughters (see page 27).

(6) Edward Backhouse, of Ashburne, Sunderland, banker, born at Darlington 9th July, 1781, died at Sunderland 7th June, 1860; married at Darlington 5th Aug., 1807, Mary, eldest daughter of Edward Robson, of that place; she died at Sunderland 23rd July, 1860, aged 71, having had 3 sons and 2 daughters (see page 31).

(7) James Backhouse, of West Lodge, Darlington, banker, born at Darlington 11th Nov., 1782, died unmarried 26th July, 1837.

(8) John Backhouse, of Darlington, banker, born there 20th March, 1784, died at Shull, 17th Aug., 1847; married, 1st, at Cork, 25th May, 1809, Eliza, 3rd and youngest daughter of Matthew Church of Cork (sister of Lieut.-Col. Sir Richard Church, G.C.H., C.B., a Field-Marshal in the Greek Army, and aunt of Dean Church); she died 2nd Sept., 1812; he married, 2ndly, 13th Aug., 1823, Katharine, 5th daughter of Jasper Capper, of Stoke Newington (and Anne Fry, his wife); she was born 16th Oct., 1792, and died *s.p.* 16th March, 1882. By his 1st wife he had a son and 2 daughters:

(1) Ann Backhouse, born 2nd May, 1810, died at Manheim, 29th May, 1829.

(2) John Church Backhouse, of Darlington, banker, born there 8th Aug., 1811, and died 10th November, 1858; married 8th Nov., 1843, Anna, daughter of Joseph John Gurney, of Earlham Hall, Norfolk, banker; she was born 21st Dec., 1820, and died at Palermo 17th Jan., 1848, having had a son and daughter:

(1) John Henry Backhouse, of Blackwell, Darlington, banker, born 22nd Oct., 1844, died 20th July, 1869.

(2) Eliza Jane Backhouse, born 23rd March, 1847, died at Pisa, 26th Nov., 1847.

(3) Eliza Backhouse, born 2nd Sept., 1812, died at Darlington 5th March, 1884; married 9th Sept., 1841, to Robert Barclay, of Leyton, Essex, and of London, banker; he died *s.p.* 4th May, 1842.

(9) Ann Backhouse, born at Darlington 28th Oct., 1785, died 7th Aug., 1852.

(10) Jane Backhouse, born at Darlington 3rd May, 1787, died 6th August, 1873; married at Darlington 3rd Aug., 1815, to Edward Robson, of Darlington (son of Edward Robson

MRS. DAVID DALE.

DAVID DALE.

EDWARD R. WHITWELL.

JAMES B. DALE.

and his wife Elizabeth Dearman). He died at Exmouth 26th Feb., 1819, aged 28, leaving an only daughter:

Ann Backhouse Robson, born at Darlington 14th March, 1817; married firstly at Darlington, 24th Sept., 1840, to Henry Whitwell, of Darlington, 6th son of Isaac Whitwell, of Kendal, where he was born 24th Oct., 1818, and died at Madrid, 27th March, 1848, leaving a son and daughter:

(1) Maria Jane Whitwell, born at Darlington 6th August, 1841, died 14th Sept., 1890; married there 21st April, 1864, to William Lucas (son of William and Elizabeth Lucas), who was born at Hitchin 22nd Jan., 1832, and had a son and daughter:

(1) William Lucas, born at Hitchin, 11th July, 1866.

(2) Helen Lucas, born at Hitchin, 13th Jan., 1868.

(2) Edward Robson Whitwell, of the Friarage, Yarm-on-Tees, J.P. co. Durham and Yorks, N.R., born at Sunderland 27th Jan., 1843; married 12th Feb., 1873, Mary Janet, daughter of Edward Aldam Leatham, Esq., of Misarden Park, co. Glouc., and has 2 sons and 3 daughters, all born at Barton Hall, Darlington:

(1) Annie Violet Whitwell, born 25th Dec., 1873.

(2) Edward Leatham Whitwell, born 17th Jan., 1875.

(3) Henry Cecil Whitwell, born 12th Nov., 1876.

(4) Janet Muriel Whitwell, born 1st Jan., 1878.

(5) Gladys Rachel Whitwell, born 12th March, 1882.

Mrs. Ann Backhouse (Whitwell) Dale, died at Darlington, 15th Sept., 1886, having married secondly, 27th Jan., 1853, as 1st wife to David Dale, of West Lodge, Darlington, J.P., D.L. co. Durham, High Sheriff 1888, and had another son and daughter:

(3) Annie Marion Stuart Dale, born 28th Nov., 1853; married 14th April, 1874, to Edward Hutchinson, of Darlington, solicitor (son of Henry and Frances Ann), *s.p.*

(4) James Backhouse Dale, of Carlbury Hall, co. Durham, J.P., born at Darlington 7th June, 1855; married 17th April, 1879, Helena, daughter of late Henry William Fenwick, of Newcastle-upon-Tyne.

JOHN
co. L

A

HANNAH BACK- = HOUSE, born 1658, died 1729.

See pa

NATHAN HUBBERSTH

JAMES BACKHOUSE, of West Lod Darlington, flax-dresser and lin manufacturer, established the ba at Darlington 1774, born 1721, di 1798. See page 17.

JONATHAN BACKHOUSE, of D born 1747, mar. 1774, died 1

D

ELIZABETH BACK- = THOMAS RIC HOUSE, born 1777, mar. 1799, died 1843. | SON, of Sunde died 1835.

See pages 17, 18.

G

JANE GURNEY BACKHOU born 1814, mar. 1844, died 18 See next page.

ROBERT FOX, of Grove Hill, Falmouth, b. 1845, m. 1867. = ELLEN MA dau. of FR CIS BASSET Heath, Le ton, Beds.

LILIAN ISABEL FOX, b. 1868, m. 1891, FREDERIC HERBERT TRENCH, Esq. =

WALLACE, b. 1892.

ROBERT BAR FOX, b. 1873.

NAOMI BA FOX, b. 1886.

Backhouse, of Darlington—Fox and Hodgkin.

JOHN BACKHOUSE, of Moss-side near Yealand Redman, co. Lanc., yeoman, died in 1690. See page 13. = SARAH, daughter of William Jackson, of Yealand Redmayne, by his wife Mabel, heiress of her brother John Carr, of Ridgend, in Mansergh, born about 1626, died 1706.

A

HANNAH BACKHOUSE, born 1658, died 1729. = JOHN CUMMING, of Hilderstone, mar. 1682, died in 1697.
See page 48.

THOMAS BACKHOUSE, of Yealand Redman, born 1661, died 1729. = ALICE, daughter of Richard Becke, of Wythmore in Westmorland, mar. 1696, died 1700.
See page 13.

SARAH BACKHOUSE, born 1664, mar. 1688, died 1697, 1st wife. = GEORGE ROBINSON, of Yealand Conyers, died 1719.
See page 14.

JAMES BACKHOUSE, of Yealand Conyers, born 1668, died in Lancaster Castle, 1697 (1st husband). See page 14. = JANET, daughter of John Godsalve, of Yealand Conyers, mar. 1691. = JOHN ROBINSON, of Yealand, mar. 1701, 2nd husband.

NATHAN HUBBERSTIE = MARY, daughter of Thomas Thornton, of Caton, co. Lanc. (J. B.'s 1st wife), mar. 1715, died 1716. = JOHN BACKHOUSE, of Hornby, born 1693, died 1739. = MARGARET (2nd wife), daughter of John and Ruth Ayrey, of Kendal, born about 1694, mar. 1720, died 1772.
See page 14.
See page 14.

WILLIAM BACKHOUSE, of Yealand, a minister of the Society of Friends, born 1696, died 1761. See page 15. = AGNES, daughter of Richard Atkinson, of Monk Coniston, born in 1697, mar. in 1720, died in 1773.

JAMES BACKHOUSE, of West Lodge, Darlington, flax-dresser and linen manufacturer, established the bank at Darlington 1774, born 1721, died 1798. See page 17. = JANE, only child of Jonathan Hedley, of Darlington, born 1718, mar. at Stockton 1746, died in 1805.

WILLIAM BACKHOUSE, born 1724, sometime of New York, died there 1792, mar. ELIZABETH, daughter of Jonathan Thornton, of Caton. She died 1750.
See page 16.

B

AGNES BACKHOUSE, born 1730, mar. 1764, died 1797. = JOHN HARRISON, of Darlington, born 1725, died 1800.
See page 39.

JOHN BACKHOUSE, of Lancaster, born 1733, died in New York 1775, mar. 1757 JANE, daughter of George Dodgson, of Kendal. She died 1763.
See page 16.

JONATHAN BACKHOUSE, of Darlington, banker, born 1747, mar. 1774, died 1826. See page 17. = ANN, 2nd daughter of Edward Pease, of Darlington, born 1746, died there in 1826.

C

JAMES BACKHOUSE, of Darlington, banker, born 1757, mar. 1787, died 1804. See page 34. = MARY, daughter of Nathan Dearman, of Thorne, Yorks, born 1764, died 24th May, 1838.

D

ELIZABETH BACKHOUSE, born 1777, mar. 1799, died 1843. = THOMAS RICHARDSON, of Sunderland, died 1835.
See pages 17, 18.

JONATHAN BACKHOUSE, of Darlington, banker, born 1779, mar. 1811, died 1842. See page 25. = HANNAH CHAPMAN, elder daughter and co-heir of Joseph Gurney, of Norwich, died 1850.

E

WILLIAM BACKHOUSE, of Darlington, banker, born 1779, died 1844, mar. 1806, MARY, daughter of John Dixon, of Cockfield. She died 1874.
See page 27.

F

EDWARD BACKHOUSE, of Sunderland, banker, born 1781, died 1860, mar. 1807, MARY, daughter of Edward Robson. She died 1860.
See page 31.

JOHN BACKHOUSE, of Darlington, banker, married twice, and died 17th Aug., 1847.
See page 22.

JANE BACKHOUSE, born 1787, mar. 1815, died 1873. = EDWARD ROBSON, of Darlington, died 1819.

ANN BACKHOUSE ROBSON, mar. 1st to HENRY WHITWELL, and 2nd to DAVID DALE. See pages, 22, 23.

G

JANE GURNEY BACKHOUSE, born 1814, mar. 1844, died 1860. See next page. = ROBERT BARCLAY FOX, of Falmouth, died 1855.

H

ANNE BACKHOUSE, born 1815, mar. 1843, died 1845. See next page. = JOHN HODGKIN, of Lewes, died in 1875.

EDMUND BACKHOUSE, of Darlington, banker and M.P. 1868-80, born 1824. See next page. = JULIET MARY, elder daughter and eventually sole heir of Charles Fox, of Trebah, Cornwall, mar. 1848.
See page 11.

ROBERT FOX, of Grove Hill, Falmouth, b. 1845, m. 1867. = ELLEN MARY, dau. of FRANCIS BASSETT, of Heath, Leighton, Beds.

- LILIAN ISABEL FOX, b. 1868, m. 1891, FREDERIC HERBERT TRENCH, Esq.
  - WALLACE, b. 1892.
- ROBERT BARCLAY FOX, b. 1873.
- NAOMI BASSETT FOX, b. 1886.

GEORGE CROKER FOX, J.P., Cornwall, b. 1847, m. 1871, ADA MARY, eldest dau. of CAPT. WAKE, R.N.

- GEORGE CROKER FOX, b. 1871.
- HEREWALD E. C. FOX, b. 1874.
- CECIL CROKER FOX, b. 1879.

HENRY BACKHOUSE FOX, b. 1849.

JOSEPH GURNEY FOX, b. 1850, m. 1873, MARGARET MAY, youngest dau. of WILLIAM JUST, Esq.

- MARGARET JANE GURNEY FOX, b. 1874.

JANE HANNAH BACKHOUSE FOX, b. 1852, m. 1881, as 2nd wife, HORATIO NOBLE PYM, of London.

- JULIET CAROLINE FOX PYM, b. 1882.
- YOLANDE SILVIA NINA NOBLE PYM, b. 1883.

JONATHAN BACKHOUSE HODGKIN, of Cleveland Lodge, Great Ayton, and of Elm Ridge, Darlington, Mayor 1884-85, b. 1843. See page 26. = MARY ANNA, younger dau. of JOHN PEASE, of Darlington, m. 24th April, 1873.

- JONATHAN EDWARD HODGKIN, b. 1875.
- HENRY THEODORE HODGKIN, b. 1877.
- HAROLD OLAF HODGKIN, b. 1879.
- ROLAND HODGKIN, b. 1880.
- MARY HODGKIN, b. 1882.

Robert Barclay Fox
1817-1855.

Jane Gurney Fox

Robert Barclay Fox

Robert Fox

Mrs Robert Fox

BACKHOUSE OF DARLINGTON.

JONATHAN BACKHOUSE, of Polam Hill, Darlington, banker, silver medallist Society of Arts, 1813, a promoter of the Stockton and Darlington Railway; he and his wife were ministers of the Society of Friends in Great Britain and North America (2nd son of Jonathan Backhouse and Ann Pease, see page 17); born at Darlington 19th Jan., 1779, died 7th October, 1842; married 23rd April, 1811, Hannah Chapman, elder daughter of Joseph Gurney, of Norwich (and co-heir with her sister Emma, wife of Joseph Pease), she was born 9th Feb., 1787, and died 6th May, 1850, having had 4 sons and 2 daughters, all born at Darlington:

(1) Jonathan Backhouse, born 5th Sept., 1812, died 7th Sept., 1820.

(2) Jane Gurney Backhouse, born 21st May, 1814, died at Pau 10th April, 1860; married 10th Oct., 1844, to Robert Barclay Fox (only son of Robert Were Fox, F.R.S., of Falmouth); he was born 6th Sept., 1817, and died at Cairo 10th March, 1855, having had 4 sons and a daughter:

- (1) Robert Fox, of Grove Hill, Falmouth, born 31st July, 1845; married 3rd Oct., 1867, Ellen Mary, daughter of Francis Bassett, of Heath, Leighton, Beds (sometime M.P.), and has a son and 2 daughters:
  - (1) Lilian Isabel Fox, born 20th Nov., 1868; married 15th July, 1891, to Frederic Herbert Trench, Examiner Education Department; B.A., from Keble College, 1888; Fellow of All Souls College, Nov., 1889; M.A. 1892; son of late William Wallace Trench, Esq. (see Foster's Peerage, B. Ashtown), and has 2 sons:
    - (1) Wallace Talbot Trench, born 11th May, 1892.
    - (2) Esmond Patrick, born 14th July, 1893.
  - (2) Robert Barclay Fox, born 24th July, 1873.
  - (3) Naomi Bassett Fox, born 1st Feb., 1886.
- (2) George Croker Fox, J.P. Cornwall, born 28th Feb., 1847; married 24th Jan., 1871, Ada Mary, eldest daughter of Baldwin Arden Wake, Capt. R.N. (see Foster's Baronetage), and has had 3 sons and 2 daughters:
  - (1) George Croker Fox, born 28th Oct., 1871.
  - (2) Myra Caroline Arden Fox, born 11th March, 1873, died 24th April, 1890.
  - (3) Herewald Evelyn Croker Fox, born 29th July, 1874.
  - (4) Cecil Croker Fox, born 14th Nov., 1879.
- (3) Henry Backhouse Fox, born 5th March, 1849.
- (4) Joseph Gurney Fox, born 9th Sept., 1850; married 9th July, 1873, Margaret May, youngest daughter of William Just, Esq., of Bankfields, Eastham, Cheshire, and has had 2 daughters:

(1) Margaret Jane Gurney Fox, born 3rd July, 1874, twin with

(2) Juliet Maud Gurney Fox, who died 1874.

(5) Jane Hannah Backhouse Fox, born 5th Nov., 1852; married 2nd May, 1881, as 2nd wife to Horatio Noble Pym, of Foxwold, Kent, (whose 1st wife was Sarah Juliet Backhouse, see page 11), and has 2 daughters:

(1) Juliet Caroline Fox Pym, born 26th March, 1882.

(2) Yolande Sylvia Nina Noble Pym, born 20th May, 1883.

(3) Ann Backhouse, born 31st Dec., 1815, died 30th Nov., 1845; married 16th Feb., 1843, as 2nd wife to John Hodgkin, of Lewes, who died (after marrying again) 5th July, 1875, aged 75 (see "Dictionary of National Biography"), leaving by her a son:

JONATHAN BACKHOUSE HODGKIN, of Cleveland Lodge, Great Ayton, and of Elm Ridge, Darlington, mayor 1884-5, born 27th Dec., 1843; married 24th April, 1873, Mary Anna, younger daughter of John Pease, of Darlington, and has 4 sons and a daughter:

(1) Jonathan Edward Hodgkin, born 4th Nov., 1875.

(2) Henry Theodore Hodgkin, born 21st April, 1877.

(3) Harold Olaf Hodgkin, born 16th April, 1879.

(4) Ronald Hodgkin, born 23rd July, 1880.

(5) Mary Hodgkin, born 20th June, 1882.

(4) Joseph Gurney Backhouse, born 19th Sept., 1817, died 23rd Nov., 1824.

(5) Henry Gurney Backhouse, born 15th July, 1819, died 16th April, 1836.

(6) EDMUND BACKHOUSE, of whom see page 11.

John Hodgkin
In 1867.

Ann Backhouse.
Second Wife.

J B Hodgkin

Mrs J B Hodgkin

William Backhouse.
1779-1844.

William Backhouse
1807-1869.

Mary (Dixon) Backhouse.
1783-1874.

Katherine (Aldam) Backhouse
1815-1868.

BACKHOUSE OF ST. JOHN'S, WOLSINGHAM.

WILLIAM BACKHOUSE, of Darlington, banker (5th child of Jonathan Backhouse, of Darlington, see page 22), born there 17th Nov., 1779, died 9th June, 1844; married 27th March, 1806, Mary, daughter of John Dixon, of Cockfield; she was born there 14th Nov., 1783, and died at Chapel Allerton, *alias* Chapeltown, near Leeds, 22nd March, 1874, aged 90, having had 5 sons and 3 daughters:

(1) William Backhouse, of St. John's, Wolsingham, and of Darlington, first chairman of the Darlington board of health, born 12th Jan., 1807, died in Leeds 3rd April, 1869; married, 1st, 13th March, 1833, Amelia, daughter of Joseph Fryer, of Rastrick, Brighouse, Yorks, she died 27th Jan., 1837, having had twin children, born 1833 and died in early infancy; he married, 2ndly, 18th Oct., 1843, Katherine Aldam Aldam, eldest daughter of William (Pease) Aldam, of Warmsworth, Yorks (and Sarah Jowitt, his wife); she was born 12th Oct., 1815, and died 27th Dec., 1868, leaving 4 sons and a daughter:

(3) William Aldam Backhouse, born 27th April, 1846.

(4) Charles James Backhouse, of St. John's, Wolsingham, co. Durham, J.P., born 4th Jan., 1848; married 28th Oct., 1874, Lucy, daughter of Major John Read Vincent, of Hemsworth, Yorkshire, no issue.

(5) Henry Backhouse, of Red House, Darlington, born 29th June, 1849; married, 1st, 16th April, 1885, Georgina Mary, 2nd daughter of John Harrison Stanton, of Stubb House, co. Durham; she died 25th July, 1890; he married, 2ndly, 29th August, 1893, Mary, elder daughter of Arthur Lucas, of Darlington. By his 1st wife he had 2 sons:

(1) John William Backhouse, born 9th March, 1886.

(2) Rowland Henry Backhouse, born 16th March, 1887, died 14th July, 1890.

(6) Sarah Aldam Backhouse, born 14th Nov., 1851, married 3rd Dec., 1874, as 2nd wife to Christopher Bowly, Esq., J.P., of Siddington House, Cirencester, *s.p.*

(7) Robert Ormston Backhouse, of Sutton Court, co. Hereford, born 10th March, 1854; married 30th April, 1884, Sarah Elizabeth, eldest daughter of William Dodgson, of Dykeside, Cumberland, and has a son:

William Ormston Backhouse, born 20th Feb., 1885.

(2) Frederick Backhouse, of Stockton-on-Tees, banker, born at Darlington 29th April, 1808, and died there 16th April, 1845; married at Wandsworth, Surrey, 5th Sept., 1833, Eliza, daughter of Samuel Fossick, of the same, and had 2 sons and a daughter:

(1) Frederick William Backhouse, of Bexhill, Hastings, sometime of London, stockbroker, born 9th Dec., 1834; married 24th Sept., 1878, Emily Ellen, eldest daughter of Rev. Paul M. Stedman, vicar of Thurston.

(2) Ann Eliza Backhouse, born at Stockton 20th Jan., 1836, died 27th Dec., 1886; married at Stockton 18th Dec., 1856, as 1st wife, to Joseph Richardson, of Potto Hall, Northallerton, J.P. Yorks, N.R.; J.P. and D.L. co. Durham, sheriff 1886; mayor of Stockton 4 times, 1886, &c.; M.P. co. Durham, S.E. division, 1892 (he married, 2ndly, 4th Sept., 1893, Flora, youngest daughter of late James Macdonald, of Birkenhead), and has had 2 sons and 5 daughters:

ACKHOUSE

BACKHOUSE

a, e 27

Backhouse, of St. John's, Wolsingham.

JOHN BACKHOUSE, of Moss-side near Yealand Redman, co. Lanc., yeoman, died in 1690. See page 13. = SARAH, daughter of William Jackson, of Yealand Redmayne, by his wife Mabel, heiress of her brother John Carr, of Ridgend, in Mansergh, born about 1626, died 1706.

A

HANNAH BACKHOUSE, born 1658, died 1729. = JOHN CUMMING, of Hilderstone, mar. 1682, died in 1697. See page 48.

THOMAS BACKHOUSE, of Yealand Redman, born 1661, died 1729. = ALICE, daughter of Richard Becke, of Wythmore in Westmorland, mar. 1696, died 1700. See page 13.

SARAH BACKHOUSE, born 1664, mar. 1688, died 1697, 1st wife. = GEORGE ROBINSON, of Yealand Conyers, died 1719. See page 14.

JAMES BACKHOUSE, of Yealand Conyers, born 1668, died in Lancaster Castle, 1697 (1st husband). See page 14. = JANET, daughter of John Godsalve, of Yealand Conyers, mar. 1691. = JOHN ROBINSON, of Yealand, mar. 1701, 2nd husband.

NATHAN HUBBERSTIE = MARY, daughter of Thomas Thornton, of Caton, co. Lanc. (J. B.'s 1st wife), mar. 1715, died 1716. = JOHN BACKHOUSE, of Hornby, born 1693, died 1739. See page 14. = MARGARET (2nd wife), daughter of John and Ruth Ayrey, of Kendal, born about 1694, mar. 1720, died 1772. See page 14.

WILLIAM BACKHOUSE, of Yealand, a minister of the Society of Friends, born 1696, died 1761. See page 15. = AGNES, daughter of Richard Atkinson, of Monk Coniston, born in 1697, mar. in 1720, died in 1773.

JAMES BACKHOUSE, of West Lodge, Darlington, flax-dresser and linen manufacturer, established the bank at Darlington 1774, born 1721, died 1798. See page 17. = JANE, only child of Jonathan Hedley, of Darlington, born 1718, mar. at Stockton 1746, died in 1805.

WILLIAM BACKHOUSE, born 1724, sometime of New York, died there 1792, mar. ELIZABETH, daughter of Jonathan Thornton, of Caton. She died 1750. See page 16.

B

AGNES BACKHOUSE, born 1730, mar. 1764, died 1797. = JOHN HARRISON, of Darlington, born 1725, died 1800. See page 39.

JOHN BACKHOUSE, of Lancaster, born 1733, died in New York 1775, mar. 1757 JANE, daughter of George Dodgson, of Kendal. She died 1763. See page 16.

JONATHAN BACKHOUSE, of Darlington, banker, born 1747, mar. 1774, died 1826. See page 17. = ANN, 2nd daughter of Edward Pease, of Darlington, born 1746, died there in 1826.

C

JAMES BACKHOUSE, of Darlington, banker, born 1757, mar. 1787, died 1804. See page 34. = MARY, daughter of Nathan Dearman, of Thorne, Yorks, born 1764, died 24th May, 1838.

D

ELIZABETH BACKHOUSE, born 1777, mar. 1799, died 1843. = THOMAS RICHARDSON, of Sunderland, died 1835. See pages 17, 18.

JONATHAN BACKHOUSE, of Darlington, banker, born 1779, mar. 1811, died 1842. = HANNAH CHAPMAN, elder daughter and co-heir of Joseph Gurney, of Norwich, died 1850. See page 25.

E

WILLIAM BACKHOUSE, of Darlington, banker, born 1779, died 1844, mar. 1806, MARY, daughter of John Dixon, of Cockfield. She died 1874.

F

EDWARD BACKHOUSE, of Sunderland, banker, born 1781, died 1860, mar. 1807, MARY, daughter of Edward Robson. She died 1860. See page 31.

JOHN BACKHOUSE, of Darlington, banker, married twice, and died 17th Aug., 1847. See page 22.

JANE BACKHOUSE, born 1787, mar. 1815, died 1873. = EDWARD ROBSON, of Darlington, died 1819.

ANN BACKHOUSE ROBSON, mar. 1st to HENRY WHITWELL, and 2nd to DAVID DALE. See pages, 22, 23.

AMELIA (1st wife), dau. of JOSEPH FRYER, of Rastrick, Brighouse, mar. 1833, died 1837. = WILLIAM BACKHOUSE, of St. John's, Wolsingham, etc., born 1807, died 1869. See page 27. = KATHERINE ALDAM ALDAM, (2nd wife), dau. of WM. ALDAM, of Warmsworth, Yorks, mar. 1843, died 1868.

FREDERICK BACKHOUSE, of Stockton-on-Tees, banker, born 1808, died 1845. See page 27. = ELIZA, dau. of SAMUEL FOSSICK, of Wandsworth, Surrey, mar. 1833.

ELIZABETH B., born 1811, died 1891, mar. 1838, HENRY BROADHEAD, of Sheepscar, Leeds, died 1882.

MARIA B., born 1814, died 1887, mar. 1843, ISAAC BIGLAND, who died in 1890.

JANE BACKHOUSE, born 1816, mar. 1843, to HODGSON BIGLAND, of Darlington.

WILLIAM ALDAM BACKHOUSE, b. 1846.
CHARLES JAMES B., born 1848, mar. 1874, LUCY VINCENT.

HENRY BACKHOUSE, of Red House, Darlington, born 1849, mar. 1885, GEORGINA M. STANTON.
JOHN WILLIAM B., born 1886.

SARAH ALDAM B., mar. 1874, CHRISTOPHER BOWLY, of Cirencester, s.p.

ROBERT ORMSTON BACKHOUSE, of Sutton Court, Hereford, born 1854, mar. 1884, SARAH ELIZABETH DODGSON.
WILLIAM ORMSTON B., born 1885.

FREDERICK WM., of Bexhill, Sussex, born 1834, mar. 1878, EMILY E. STEDMAN.
ANN ELIZA B., died 1886, mar. 1856, to JOSEPH RICHARDSON, of Potto Hall, Northallerton.
See pages 29, 30.

HENRIETTA BROADHEAD, mar. 1862, EDWARD PRIESTMAN, of Leeds, and has issue. See page 29.
WM. HENRY BROADHEAD, born 1841, mar. 1878, HANNAH MARIA BRIGHTWEN, and has issue. See pages 29, 30.

ANN BIGLAND, born 1848.
ISAAC B., born 1853.
HERBERT BIGLAND, born 1858, mar. 1878, MARY STEWART.
See page 30.

MARY B. BIGLAND, born 1844.
WILLIAM B., died s.p. 1885.
JANE, born 1847.
CHARLES H., born 1851, mar. MARY E. DAVISON, and has issue. See p. 30.
ANNE H., born 1859.
FANNY, born 1861.

William A. Backhouse.
See Page 27.

Charles J. Backhouse.

Mrs Bowly.

Henry Backhouse.

Robert O. Backhouse.
See Page 27.

Frederick W. Backhouse
See Page 27.

Mrs F. W. Backhouse
See Page 27.

Mrs Frederick Backhouse
See Page 27.

Mrs J. Richardson
1836-1886.
See Page 27.

INK PHOTO. SPRAGUE & C°. LONDON

(1) Frederick Backhouse Richardson, born at Norton, 16th Nov., 1857, died 10th Aug., 1859.

(2) Frances Mary Richardson, born at Norton 12th April, 1859; married 21st April, 1892, to Rev. Charles Hutton Coates, M.A., late chaplain Royal Navy, vicar of Sand Hutton, Yorks, youngest son of James Coates, Esq., J.P., of Helperby Hall, Yorks.

(3) Annie Backhouse Richardson, born at Norton 16th Nov., 1860; married 24th April, 1884, to Alfred Edward Kitching, of Great Ayton, J.P., D.L., Yorks, N.R., and has a son and daughter:

(1) Harold Edward Kitching, born 31st Aug., 1885.

(2) Amy Maud Kitching, born 2nd Oct., 1887.

(4) Amy Louisa Richardson, born at Norton 18th March, 1862.

(5) Edith Richardson, born at Woodlands, Stockton, 20th July, 1864, and died 3rd Aug. following.

(6) Marion Josephine Richardson, born at Woodlands, Stockton, 2nd June, 1866; married 26th November, 1891, to Cecil Wagner Holms, of Leicester (2nd son of Major Holms, of Grey Towers, Hornchurch, Essex), and has a son:

Eric Cecil Holms, born 18th Oct., 1892.

(7) Edwin Backhouse Richardson, born at Woodlands, Stockton, 22nd May, 1869.

(3) James Backhouse, born at Stockton, 13th May, 1837, died 10th Jan., 1838.

(3) Jonathan Backhouse, born at Darlington 26th Dec., 1809, died 12th Sept., 1834.

(4) Elizabeth Backhouse, born at Darlington 30th April, 1811, died 28th March, 1891; married there 28th Sept., 1838, to Henry Broadhead, of Sheepscar, Leeds, oil merchant, and latterly of Chapel Allerton; he died 25th February, 1882, aged 80, having had 2 sons and a daughter:

(1) Henrietta Broadhead, born 7th July, 1839; married at Leeds 12th June, 1862, to Edward Priestman, of Bradford (son of John, of Bradford), and had 4 sons and 3 daughters:

(1) George Edward Priestman, born 27th October, 1863; married , 1890, Maude Mallory, and has a son:

Kenneth Priestman, born , 1891.

(2) Howard Priestman, born 22nd Dec., 1865.

(3) Bertram Priestman, born 30th Nov., 1868.

(4) Gertrude Priestman, born 7th Nov., 1870.

(5) Helen Maud Priestman, born 26th Feb., 1872.

(6) Henrietta Ada Priestman, born 3rd June, 1874.

(7) Harold Priestman, born 6th Oct., 1878.

(2) William Henry Broadhead, of Ilkley, born 1st Aug., 1841; married at Scarborough, 31st July, 1878, Hannah Maria, second daughter of Charles and Hannah (Rowntree) Brightwen, of Newcastle-on-Tyne, and has 2 sons and 2 daughters:

(1) Florence Elizabeth Broadhead, born 14th Aug., 1879.
(2) William Edward Broadhead, born 7th March, 1881.
(3) Henrietta Maria Broadhead, born 26th April, 1883.
(4) Norman Henry Broadhead, born 25th Aug., 1885.

(3) Edward Broadhead, born 27th Aug., 1844; died at Chapel Allerton, *alias* Chapeltown, near Leeds, 6th July, 1877.

(5) Maria Backhouse, born 20th Oct., 1814, died 3rd Nov., 1887; married at Darlington 14th Dec., 1843, to Isaac Bigland, sometime of Everton, woollen draper, of Lintz Green, co. Durham, and of Newcastle-upon-Tyne; he died at Stockton-on-Tees 18th Jan., 1890, having had 2 sons and a daughter:

(1) Anne Bigland, born 4th Oct., 1848.
(2) Isaac Henry Bigland, born 1st June, 1853.
(3) Herbert Bigland, of Middlesboro, solicitor, born 20th July, 1858; married at Redcar 1878, Mary, daughter of John Stewart, of Stockton-upon-Tees, and has had 2 sons and 3 daughters, all born at Middlesboro:

(1) Arthur Herbert Bigland, born 11th April, 1879.
(2) Laura Maria Bigland, born 4th July, 1883.
(3) Mabel Mary Bigland, born 11th June, 1886.
(4) Eleanor Bigland, born 23rd April, 1888, died 26th June following.
(5) Ronald Cecil Bigland, born 21st Oct., 1889.

(6) Jane Backhouse, born 10th Oct., 1816, died 2nd Dec., 1888, having married 23rd Feb., 1843, to Hodgson Bigland, of Liverpool, and had 4 sons and 6 daughters:

(1) Mary Backhouse Bigland, born 22nd Feb., 1844.
(2) William Backhouse Bigland, born 1st Aug., 1845, died *s.p.* 26th Dec., 1885; married 20th Dec., 1881, Isabella Wilson.
(3) Jane Bigland, born 26th May, 1847.
(4) Frederick Bigland, born 24th June, 1849, died 12th Jan., 1867.
(5) Charles Hodgson Bigland, of Oxton, Cheshire, born 9th May, 1851; married 2nd May, 1879, Mary Elizabeth, daughter of William Hodgson Davison, and has a son and 3 daughters:

(1) Daisy Bigland, born 27th Jan., 1881.
(2) Elsie Bigland, born 4th Aug., 1886.
(3) Lilian Bigland, born 9th July, 1887.
(4) Frederick Bigland, born 28th Jan., 1889.

(6) Lucy Bigland, born 16th May, 1853, died 12th March, 1859.
(7) Katharine Bigland, born 2nd June, 1855, died 15th March, 1859.
(8) Jonathan Bigland, born 26th July, 1857, died 24th Feb., 1880.
(9) Anne Hodgson Bigland, born 4th Feb., 1859.
(10) Fanny Bigland, born 9th Sept., 1861.

(7) Charles John Backhouse, born 1st Aug., 1819, died 28th Nov., 1820.
(8) James Backhouse, born 11th March, 1822, died 27th Oct., 1826.

EDWARD BACKHOUSE
1781-1860.
See Page 31.

MARY BACKHOUSE
Died, 1860.
See Page 31.

ELIZABETH RICHARDSON
1777-1843.
See Page 17.

JANE ROBSON
1787-1873.
See Page 22.

EDWARD BACKHOUSE
1808-1879.

MRS E BACKHOUSE

ALFRED BACKHOUSE
1822-1888

MRS A BACKHOUSE.

BACKHOUSE OF SUNDERLAND.

EDWARD BACKHOUSE, of Ashburne, Sunderland, J.P., banker (4th son of Jonathan Backhouse, of Darlington, banker, see page 22); received in 1814 the gold medal of the Society for the encouragement of Arts, Manufactures, and Commerce; born at Darlington 9th July, 1781, died at Sunderland 7th June, 1860; married at Darlington 5th Aug., 1807, Mary, eldest daughter of Edward Robson, of that place; she died at Sunderland 23rd July, 1860, aged 71, having had 3 sons and 2 daughters:

(1) Edward Backhouse, of Ashburne, Sunderland, banker and philanthropist, author of "Early Church History," a minister in the Society of Friends, born at Darlington 8th May, 1808, died *s.p.* at Hastings 22nd May, 1879 (see "Dictionary of National Biography"); he married 26th March, 1856, Katharine, daughter of Thomas Mounsey, of Sunderland.

(2) THOMAS JAMES BACKHOUSE, of whom presently.

(3) Lucy Backhouse Backhouse, born at Darlington 16th December, 1812, died 30th March, 1872; married 24th July, 1839, to John Mounsey, of Hendon Hill, Sunderland (2nd son of John Mounsey, by his wife, Ann Robson); he died 6th July, 1879, aged 78, having had 2 sons and 3 daughters, all born at Sunderland:

- **(1)** Edward Backhouse Mounsey, of Blackwell, Darlington, and Seaton Carew, co. Durham, banker, born at Sunderland 20th June, 1840; married at Bishop Auckland 20th Feb., 1878, Rachel Ann, youngest and only surviving daughter of Joseph Jowitt Fryer, of Holly Bank, Rastrick, Yorks, and has 3 sons and 2 daughters:
  - **(1)** John Edward Mounsey, born at Tees Grange, Darlington, 6th Dec., 1879.
  - **(2)** George Fryer Mounsey, born " " 9th Feb., 1881.
  - **(3)** Lucy Backhouse Mounsey, born " " 10th March, 1882.
  - **(4)** Reginald Joseph Mounsey, born " " 23rd Jan., 1884.
  - **(5)** Amelia Eliza Mounsey, born at Blackwell, Darlington, 13th Oct., 1886.
- **(2)** Lucy Elizabeth Mounsey, born 27th Nov., 1841.
- **(3)** John Wilfred Mounsey, of Sunderland, born there 7th Oct., 1843; married 13th May, 1868, Mary Charlotte, 2nd daughter of Joshua Green, of Stanstead, Essex (by his wife Elizabeth Robson), and has 2 sons and a daughter, all born at Sunderland:
  - **(1)** Ethel Mary Mounsey, born 4th Sept., 1869.
  - **(2)** Wilfred Arthur Mounsey, born 13th Aug., 1871.
  - **(3)** John Harold Mounsey, born 13th Jan., 1874.
- **(4)** Anna Priscilla Mounsey, born 23rd Feb., 1847, died 4th May, 1889.
- **(5)** Mary Emma Mounsey, born 12th May, 1851.

(4) Alfred Backhouse, of Pilmore Hall and Dryderdale, co. Durham, J.P., High Sheriff 1883, and of Darlington, banker, born at Sunderland 28th Sept., 1822, died *s.p.* 2nd Sept., 1888; married 8th May, 1851, Rachel, daughter of Robert Barclay, of Knotts Green, Essex.

Backhouse, of Sunderland.

JOHN BACKHOUSE, of Moss-side near Yealand Redman, co. Lanc., yeoman, died in 1690. See page 13. = SARAH, daughter of William Jackson, of Yealand Redmayne, by his wife Mabel, heiress of her brother John Carr, of Ridgend, in Mansergh, born about 1626, died 1706.

A. HANNAH BACKHOUSE, born 1658, died 1729. = JOHN CUMMING, of Hilderstone, mar. 1682, died in 1697. See page 48.

THOMAS BACKHOUSE, of Yealand Redman, born 1661, died 1729. = ALICE, daughter of Richard Becke, of Wythmore in Westmorland, mar. 1696, died 1700. See page 13.

SARAH BACKHOUSE, born 1664, mar. 1688, died 1697, 1st wife. = GEORGE ROBINSON, of Yealand Conyers, died 1719. See page 14.

JAMES BACKHOUSE, of Yealand Conyers, born 1668, died in Lancaster Castle, 1697 (1st husband). See page 14. = JANET, daughter of John Godsalve, of Yealand Conyers, mar. 1691. = JOHN ROBINSON, of Yealand, mar. 1701, 2nd husband.

* NATHAN HUBBERSTIE = MARY, daughter of Thomas Thornton, of Caton, co. Lanc. (J. B.'s 1st wife), mar. 1715, died 1716. = JOHN BACKHOUSE, of Hornby, born 1693, died 1739. See page 14. = MARGARET (2nd wife), daughter of John and Ruth Ayrey, of Kendal, born about 1694, mar. 1720, died 1772. See page 14.

WILLIAM BACKHOUSE, of Yealand, a minister of the Society of Friends, born 1696, died 1761. See page 15. = AGNES, daughter of Richard Atkinson, of Monk Coniston, born in 1697, mar. in 1720, died in 1773.

JAMES BACKHOUSE, of West Lodge, Darlington, flax-dresser and linen manufacturer, established the bank at Darlington 1774, born 1721, died 1798. See page 17. = JANE, only child of Jonathan Hedley, of Darlington, born 1718, mar. at Stockton 1746, died in 1805.

WILLIAM BACKHOUSE, born 1724, sometime of New York, died there 1792, mar. ELIZABETH, daughter of Jonathan Thornton, of Caton. She died 1750. See page 16.

B. AGNES BACKHOUSE, born 1730, mar. 1764, died 1797. = JOHN HARRISON, of Darlington, born 1725, died 1800. See page 39.

JOHN BACKHOUSE, of Lancaster, born 1733, died in New York 1775, mar. 1757 JANE, daughter of George Dodgson, of Kendal. She died 1763. See page 16.

JONATHAN BACKHOUSE, of Darlington, banker, born 1747, mar. 1774, died 1826. See page 17. = ANN, 2nd daughter of Edward Pease, of Darlington, born 1746, died there in 1826.

C. JAMES BACKHOUSE, of Darlington, banker, born 1757, mar. 1787, died 1804. See page 34. = MARY, daughter of Nathan Dearman, of Thorne, Yorks, born 1764, died 24th May, 1838.

D. ELIZABETH BACKHOUSE, born 1777, mar. 1799, died 1843. = THOMAS RICHARDSON, of Sunderland, died 1835. See pages 17 and 18.

JONATHAN BACKHOUSE, of Darlington, banker, born 1779, mar. 1811, died 1842. = HANNAH CHAPMAN, elder daughter and co-heir of Joseph Gurney, of Norwich, died 1850. See page 25.

E. WILLIAM BACKHOUSE, of Darlington, banker, born 1779, died 1844, mar. 1806, MARY, daughter of John Dixon, of Cockfield. She died 1874. See page 27.

F. EDWARD BACKHOUSE, of Sunderland, banker, born 1781, died 1860, mar. 1807, MARY, daughter of Edward Robson. She died 1860.

JOHN BACKHOUSE, of Darlington, banker, married twice, and died 17th Aug., 1847. See page 22.

JANE BACKHOUSE, born 1787, mar. 1815, died 1873. = EDWARD ROBSON, of Darlington, died 1819.

ANN BACKHOUSE ROBSON, mar. 1st to HENRY WHITWELL, and 2nd to DAVID DALE. See pages 22 and 23.

EDWARD BACKHOUSE, of Sunderland, banker, mar. 1856, KATHARINE, dau. of THOMAS MOUNSEY, of Sunderland, and died s.p. 1879. See page 31.

THOMAS JAMES BACKHOUSE, of Sunderland, born 1810, died 1857. See page 33. = MARGARET (1st wife), only daughter of WILLIAM RICHARDSON, of North Shields, mar. 1841, died 1854.

LUCY BACKHOUSE BACKHOUSE, died 1872, mar. 1839, JOHN MOUNSEY, of Sunderland, who died 1879. See page 31.

ALFRED BACKHOUSE, of Pilmore Hall, and Dryderdale, co. Durham, mar. 1851, RACHEL, dau. of ROBERT BARCLAY, and died s.p. 1888. See page 33.

EMILY BACKHOUSE, mar. 1847 (as 1st wife), EDWARD MOUNSEY, now of Montreux, Switzerland, and died 1869. See page 33.

THOMAS WILLIAM BACKHOUSE, of West Hendon House, Sunderland, coal-owner, born 1842. See page 33.
MARY AGNES, died 1893.

JAMES EDWARD BACKHOUSE, of Hurworth Grange, co. Durham, born 1845. See page 33. = ELIZABETH BARCLAY, dau. of HENRY FOWLER, of Woodford, Essex, mar. 1873.

ARTHUR, born 1853.

EDITH MARY B., born 1874.
EDWARD B., born 1876.
MABEL B., born 1878.
[illegible]
[illegible]
BASIL HENRY B., born 1882.
JENNETT RACHEL B., born 1883.
KENNETH JAMES B., born 1885.
[illegible]
[illegible]

EDWARD BACKHOUSE MOUNSEY, of Darlington, born 1840, mar. 1878, RACHEL ANN, dau. of JOSEPH J. FRYER, of Rastrick.

JOHN EDWARD M., born 1879.
GEORGE FRYER M., born 1881.
LUCY BACKHOUSE M., born 1882.
[illegible] M., born 1884.
[illegible]

LUCY E. M., born 1841.

JOHN WILFRED MOUNSEY, of Sunderland, born 1843, mar. 1868, MARY CHARLOTTE, dau. of JOSHUA GREEN, of Stanstead, Essex.

ETHEL MARY M., born 1869.
WILFRED ARTHUR M., born 1871.
JOHN HAROLD M., [illegible]

MARY E. M., born 1851.

THOMAS EDWARD M., born 1848.
ADA MARY M., born 1849.
ELIZABETH L. M., born 1852.

MARGARET BACKHOUSE.
First wife, died 1854.
See Page 33.

THOMAS JAMES BACKHOUSE.
1810-1857.
See Page 33.

ANNE BACKHOUSE.
Second wife of T. J. Backhouse.
See Page 33.

THOMAS WILLIAM BACKHOUSE.
See Page 33.

INK PHOTO. SPRAGUE & CO. LONDON

James Edward Backhouse

Mrs J. E. Backhouse

Mary Agnes Backhouse
1844-1892.

Arthur Backhouse

(5) Emily Backhouse, born at Sunderland 29th July, 1824, died at St. Leonards 19th March, 1869; married 29th April, 1847, as 1st wife to Edward Mounsey, of Montreux, Switzerland, sometime of Sunderland; (he re-married, 1873, to Emilie Hoffherr,) and had a son and 2 daughters, who survive, and one child that died in infancy:

- (1) Thomas Edward Mounsey, born at Newcastle-upon-Tyne 26th June, 1848.
- (2) Ada Mary Mounsey, born at Newcastle-upon-Tyne 24th Oct., 1849.
- (3) , born and died 1851.
- (4) Elizabeth Laura Mounsey, born at Sunderland 20th Sept., 1852.

THOMAS JAMES BACKHOUSE, of West Hendon House, Sunderland, coal owner, born at Darlington 24th April, 1810, died in his father's lifetime at Seaton Carew 29th July, 1857; he married, 1st, 18th Aug., 1841, Margaret, only daughter of William Richardson, of North Shields (by his 2nd wife Margaret Robson); she died at Darlington, 27th March, 1854, aged 36; and he married, 2ndly, at Sunderland, 22nd Nov., 1855, Anne, daughter of Thomas Robson, of Sunderland (by his wife Anne Capper); she died 16th March, 1869, aged 59. By his 1st wife he had 4 sons and 3 daughters, all born at Sunderland:

(1) Thomas William Backhouse, of West Hendon House, Sunderland, coal owner, born 14th Aug., 1842.

(2) Mary Agnes Backhouse, born 4th Feb., 1844, died at Torquay 29th May, 1893.

(3) James Edward Backhouse, of Hurworth Grange, Darlington, co. Durham, J.P., banker, born 18th May, 1845; married 2nd Oct., 1873, Elizabeth Barclay, eldest daughter of Henry Fowler, of Woodford, Essex, and has 4 sons and 6 daughters, all (but the eldest) born at Hurworth:

- (1) Edith Mary Backhouse, born at Darlington 31st July, 1874.
- (2) Edward Backhouse, born 26th Oct., 1876.
- (3) Mabel Backhouse, born 11th Feb., 1878.
- (4) Alfred Ernest Backhouse, born 12th June, 1879.
- (5) Elspeth Lilian Backhouse, born 31st Aug., 1880.
- (6) Basil Henry Backhouse, born 9th Sept., 1882.
- (7) Jennett Rachel Backhouse, born 15th Nov., 1883.
- (8) Kenneth James Backhouse, born 26th April, 1885.
- (9) Margaret Ann Backhouse, born 4th May, 1887.
- (10) Rhoda Jane Backhouse, born 17th June, 1889.

(4) Jonathan Backhouse, born 28th Aug., 1846, died 16th Aug., 1855.

(5) Edith Margaret Backhouse, born 2nd May, 1848, died 28th Sept., 1863.

(6) Lilias Backhouse, born 4th Oct., 1849, died 5th Aug., 1852.

(7) Arthur Backhouse, born 30th Dec., 1853.

BACKHOUSE OF YORK.

The coat of arms depicted at the beginning of this family history cannot be borne of right by any branch of the family set forth under this heading.

JAMES BACKHOUSE, of West Lodge, Darlington, flax dresser and linen manufacturer, and, in conjunction with his sons, established the bank at Darlington in 1774; (see page 17) born at Yealand 1729, i. 22, died at Darlington 1st April, 1798; married at Stockton 1746, ii. 8, Jane, only child of Jonathan Hedley, of Darlington; she was born there 1718, xii. 27, and died 27th May, 1805, having had 2 sons:

(1) JONATHAN BACKHOUSE, of whom see page 17.

(2) James Backhouse, of Darlington, banker, born there 1757, vi. 29, died there 18th Dec., 1804; married 8th June, 1787, Mary, daughter of Nathan Dearman, of Thorpe, after of Pindar Oaks, Darfield, Yorks; she died at York 24th May, 1838, aged 74, having had 4 sons and 6 daughters:

(1) Nathan Backhouse, born 28th March, 1788, and died at Darlington 9th Nov., 1805.

(2) Jane Backhouse, born at Darlington 21st Jan., 1790, died at York unmarried 23rd March, 1818.

(3) Thomas Backhouse, of York, a partner with his brother James; an original director of the York, Newcastle and Berwick; York and North Midland railways, and of the Northumberland and Durham District bank, and a director and one of the founders of the York City and County bank; born at Darlington 15th June, 1792, died at York 21st March, 1845; married 1st, 27th April, 1826, Hannah, daughter of William Stickney, of Beverley (and sister of Mrs. Sarah Stickney Ellis, the authoress); she was born 15th Feb., 1796, and died 23rd Dec., 1827, leaving an only daughter:

(1) Mary Backhouse, born at York 7th Nov., 1827, died 26th Jan., 1867; married at York 1st Oct., 1851, as 1st wife to William Farrer Ecroyd, [1] of Lomeshaye, co. Lanc., J.P., of Credenhill Park, co. Hereford, J.P., D.L., lord of the manor of Credenhill, and of Whitbarrow Lodge, Westmorland; contested Carlisle 1874, North East Lancashire 1880, M.P. Preston 1881-5, and the Rossendale Division of Lancashire 1885; and has had 3 sons and 6 daughters:

(1) Edith Mary Ecroyd, born 16th Jan., 1853.

(2) Margaret Ecroyd, born 19th June, 1854, married 8th Jan., 1879, to Harry Tunstill, of Montford, near Burnley, co. Lanc., J.P., and has a son and 6 daughters:

(1) Mary Cicely Tunstill, born 15th Feb., 1880.

(2) Harry Gilbert Tunstill, born 3rd August, 1881.

[1] ARMS.—Azure, on a chevron erminois between three stags' heads erased of the last, in the centre chief point a bezant charged with a rose gules barbed and seeded proper, two oak branches slipped chevron-wise also proper. CREST.—On a wreath of the colours, in front of a demi-tower proper, thereon a stag's head erased erminois, three spears one in pale and two in saltire also proper.

Mary (Backhouse) Ecroyd
First wife, 1827-1867.

William Farrer Ecroyd.

Edith Mary Ecroyd

Thomas Backhouse Ecroyd
See Page 36.

Henry Broadhead
1802-1882.
See Page 29

Elizabeth Broadhead
1811-1891.

Henrietta Priestman

W. H. Broadhead
See Pages 29-30.

Edward Broadhead
1844-1877.
See Page 30.

(3) Margaret Farrer Tunstill, born 8th March, 1883.

883, to
ghters :

882, to
and 2

, 1837,
Wilkins

JAME
Darli
niann
at Da
1798.

en, 5th
kefield,

[35]

Jo
bo

HA
WI
Be
d.

revear,
aughter
ters :

MARY
d. 1867,
WILLIA
M.P., I

h May,
own, of

enzance

Backhouse, of York.

JOHN BACKHOUSE, of Moss-side near Yealand Redman, co. Lanc., yeoman, died in 1690. See page 13. = SARAH, daughter of William Jackson, of Yealand Redmayne, by his wife Mabel, heiress of her brother John Carr, of Ridgend, in Mansergh, born about 1626, died 1706.

A

HANNAH BACKHOUSE, born 1658, died 1729. = JOHN CUMMING, of Hilderstone, mar. 1682, died in 1697. See page 48.

THOMAS BACKHOUSE, of Yealand Redman, born 1661, died 1729. = ALICE, daughter of Richard Becke, of Wythmore in Westmorland, mar. 1696, died 1700. See page 13.

SARAH BACKHOUSE, born 1664, mar. 1688, died 1697, 1st wife. = GEORGE ROBINSON, of Yealand Conyers, died 1719. See page 14.

JAMES BACKHOUSE, of Yealand Conyers, born 1668, died in Lancaster Castle, 1697 (1st husband). See page 14. = JANET, daughter of John Godsalve, of Yealand Conyers, mar. 1691. = JOHN ROBINSON, of Yealand, mar. 1701, 2nd husband.

NATHAN HUBBERSTIE = MARY, daughter of Thomas Thornton, of Caton, co. Lanc. (J. B.'s 1st wife), mar. 1715, died 1716. = JOHN BACKHOUSE, of Hornby, born 1693, died 1739. See page 14. = MARGARET (2nd wife), daughter of John and Ruth Ayrey, of Kendal, born about 1694, mar. 1720, died 1772. See page 14.

WILLIAM BACKHOUSE, of Yealand, a minister of the Society of Friends, born 1696, died 1761. See page 15. = AGNES, daughter of Richard Atkinson, of Monk Coniston, born in 1697, mar. in 1720, died in 1773.

JAMES BACKHOUSE, of West Lodge, Darlington, flax-dresser and linen manufacturer, established the bank at Darlington 1774, born 1721, died 1798. See page 17. = JANE, only child of Jonathan Hedley, of Darlington, born 1718, mar. at Stockton 1746, died in 1805.

WILLIAM BACKHOUSE, born 1724, sometime of New York, died there 1792, mar. ELIZABETH, daughter of Jonathan Thornton, of Caton. She died 1750. See page 16.

B

AGNES BACKHOUSE, born 1730, mar. 1764, died 1797. = JOHN HARRISON, of Darlington, born 1725, died 1800. See page 39.

JOHN BACKHOUSE, of Lancaster, born 1733, died in New York 1775, mar. 1757 JANE, daughter of George Dodgson, of Kendal. She died 1763. See page 16.

JONATHAN BACKHOUSE, of Darlington, banker, born 1747, mar. 1774, died 1826. See page 17. = ANN, 2nd daughter of Edward Pease, of Darlington, born 1746, died there in 1826.

C

JAMES BACKHOUSE, of Darlington, banker, born 1757, mar. 1787, died 1804. See page 34. = MARY, daughter of Nathan Dearman, of Thorne, Yorks, born 1764, died 24th May, 1838.

HANNAH (1st wife) dau. of WILLIAM STICKNEY, of Beverley, b. 1796, m. 1826, d. 1827. = THOMAS BACKHOUSE, of York, botanist, b. 1792, d. 1845. See page 34. = ABIGAIL (2nd wife), dau. of WILLIAM DENT, of Marr, near Doncaster, m. 1837, d. 1841.

JAMES BACKHOUSE, of York, botanist, a minister of Society of Friends, b. 1794, d. 1869. See page 37. = DEBORAH, dau. of RICHARD LOWE, of Worcester, b. 1793, m. 1822, d. 1827.

JOSEPH BACKHOUSE, of Gainford, b. 1798, m. 1825, d. 1881. = MARY ANN, dau. of JOHN HOLMES, of Tivetshall Hall, Norfolk, b. 1791, d. 1874.

MARY BACKHOUSE, b. 1827, d. 1867, m. 1851 (as 1st wife), WILLIAM FARRER ECROYD, M.P., Preston, 1881-85. See page 34.

SARAH JANE BACKHOUSE, b. 1838, m. 1866, THOMAS BURTT, of Malton. See page 36.

THOMAS BACKHOUSE, only son, b. 1840, d. 1889. See page 36. = ELLEN PATIENCE, dau. of JOSIAH CROGGON, m. 1863.

ELIZABETH BACKHOUSE, b. 1822, d. 1852, m. 1847, 1st wife, JOSEPH CROSFIELD, of West Derby, co. Lanc. See page 37.

JAMES BACKHOUSE, of York, botanist, and a minister of the Society of Friends, b. 1825, d. 1890. = MARY, only dau. of ISAAC ROBSON, of Dalton, Huddersfield, m. 1855.

JANE ELIZA BACKHOUSE, only surviving dau., b. 1827, m. 1862, WILLIAM SIMPSON. See page 38.

MARY BACKHOUSE, b. 1865, m. to Rev. ALEX. BROWN, M.A.
ALICE M. BACKHOUSE, b. 1867.
ANNE M. BACKHOUSE, b. 1868.

CHARLES FENWICK BACKHOUSE, b. 1869.
HELEN CHRISTINE BACKHOUSE, b. 1870.
THOMAS ROLAND BACKHOUSE, b. 1874.

PAUL F. C. BACKHOUSE, b. 1878.
HAROLD G. S. BACKHOUSE, b. 1884.

MARY LOUISA BACKHOUSE, b. 1857.

JAMES BACKHOUSE, of York, b. 1861, m. 1890. See page 37. = MABEL GRACE, dau. of WALTER ROBSON, of Saffron Walden.

JAMES BACKHOUSE, b. 1892.

(3) Margaret Farrer Tunstill, born 8th March, 1883.
(4) Edith Dorothea Tunstill, born 8th Nov., 1884.
(5) Rosamond Tunstill, born 23rd Nov., 1885.
(6) Alice Ecroyd Tunstill, born 26th Feb., 1887.
(7) Gertrude Adelaide Tunstill, born 26th June, 1891.

(3) Gertrude Ecroyd, born 28th March, 1856, married 30th May, 1883, to William Harry Hartley, of Colne, co. Lanc., and has a son and 2 daughters:

(1) Christopher Hartley, born 22nd August, 1886.
(2) Margaret Hartley, born 25th March, 1888.
(3) Susan Moon Hartley, born 8th June, 1889.

(4) Thomas Backhouse Ecroyd, born 7th July, 1857.

(5) Alizon Ecroyd, born 4th March, 1859, married 21st June, 1882, to William Cecil Slingsby, of Carleton in Craven, Yorks, and has a son and 2 daughters:

(1) Katharine Slingsby, born 17th July, 1883.
(2) William Ecroyd Slingsby, born 2nd July, 1885.
(3) Alizon Mary Slingsby, born 7th Sept., 1888.

(6) William Ecroyd, born 28th Feb., 1861.
(7) Mary Ecroyd, born 13th Oct., 1862, died 10th Oct., 1863.
(8) Edward Ecroyd, born 9th Oct., 1864.
(9) Adelaide Jane Ecroyd, born 30th Nov., 1866.

THOMAS BACKHOUSE (3), of York, married 2ndly at Doncaster 13th April, 1837, Abigail, eldest daughter of William Dent, of Marr, near Doncaster (by Sarah Wilkins his wife); she died 7th May, 1841, leaving a son and daughter:

(2) Sarah Jane Backhouse, born 3rd Nov., 1838, married at Little Marsden, 5th Sept., 1866, to Thomas Burtt, of The Brows, Malton, formerly of Wakefield, and has 2 sons and a daughter:

(1) Edwin Burtt, born 4th July, 1867.
(2) Arthur Henry Burtt, born 8th Jan., 1869.
(3) Mary Jane Burtt, born 4th Feb., 1873.

(3) Thomas Backhouse, only son, born 13th August, 1840, died at Trevear, Penzance, 4th Jan., 1889; married 16th Sept., 1863, Ellen Patience, daughter of Josiah Croggon, of Grampound, Cornwall, and had 5 sons and 6 daughters:

(1) Thomas Backhouse, born 1864, died 1866.

(2) Mary Backhouse, born 19th Sept., 1865, married at Penzance 30th May, 1893, to Rev. Alexander Brown, M.A., only son of William J. Brown, of Dingle Priory, Liverpool.

(3) Alice Maude Backhouse, born 3rd Feb., 1867; married at Penzance 17th April, 1892, to George Haye, of Wokingham, Solicitor.

Thomas Backhouse
1840-1889.

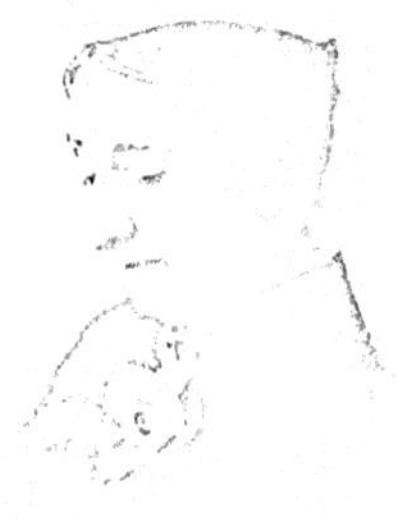

Ellen P., wife of late T. Backhouse

Mrs Alexander Brown.

Charles F. Backhouse
See Page 37.

INK-PHOTO. SPRAGUE & CO. LONDON

JAMES BACKHOUSE
1794-1869.

JAMES BACKHOUSE
1825-1890.
See Page 38.

MRS JAMES BACKHOUSE

JAMES BACKHOUSE,
Of York.
See Page 38.

(4) Annie Muriel Backhouse, born 30th May, 1868.
(5) Charles Fenwick Backhouse, born 21st June, 1869.
(6) Helen Christine Backhouse, born 20th Aug., 1870.
(7) Edith Lilian Backhouse, born 17th May, 1872, died 23rd Aug. following.
(8) Thomas Roland Backhouse, born 14th March, 1874.
(9) Paul Farrer Croggon Backhouse, born 25th May, 1878.
(10) Dorothea Backhouse, born 9th and died 26th Sept., 1882.
(11) Harold Godfrey Stephen Backhouse, born 26th April, 1884.

(4) James Backhouse, of York, a well-known practical botanist, became a minister of the Society of Friends in 1824, and in that capacity visited the Mauritius, Cape Colony, and Van Dieman's Land, &c., 1831-41; he also subsequently visited Norway; author of "A Narrative of a Visit to the Australian Colonies," and of "A Visit to the Mauritius and South Africa," &c.; born at Darlington 8th July, 1794, and died at Holgate Ho., York, 20th January, 1869; married 5th Nov., 1822, Deborah, daughter of Richard Lowe, of Worcester; she was born there 29th Aug., 1793, and died 10th Dec., 1827, having had a son and 2 daughters:

(1) Elizabeth Backhouse, born at York, 4th Aug., 1823, died 22nd April, 1852; married at York 18th Aug., 1847, as first wife to Joseph Crosfield, of Liverpool, tea dealer (son of George, of Liverpool), who died 15th Dec., 1879, aged 58, and had 3 sons and a daughter.

(1) James Backhouse Crosfield, born 25th May, 1848.

(2) George Theodore Crosfield, born 3rd August, 1849; married 30th March, 1876, Mary, daughter of Thomas Day Green, of Saffron Walden, and has a son and daughter:

(1) Alice Mary Crosfield, born 27th May, 1877.
(2) Hugh Theodore Crosfield, born 1st. June, 1883.

(3) Josephine Crosfield, born 20th January, 1851; married 2nd June, 1881, to Joseph Gundry Alexander, and has 4 sons:

(1) Gilbert Crosfield Alexander, born 2nd March, 1882.
(2) Wilfrid Backhouse Alexander, born 4th February, 1885.
(3) Christopher James Alexander, born 24th March, 1887.
(4) Horace Gundry Alexander, born 18th April, 1889.

(4) Albert Joseph Crosfield, born 14th April, 1852; married 16th Sept., 1880, Gulielma Wallis, and has had 3 sons and a daughter:

(1) Bertram Fothergill Crosfield, born 14th Nov., 1882.
(2) Raymond Arthur Crosfield, born 2nd Dec., 1884, and died 22nd May, 1885.
(3) Albert Ronald Crosfield, born 1st June, 1886.
(4) Hilda Margaret Crosfield, born 27th June, 1888.

(2) James Backhouse, of West Bank, Holgate, York, practical botanist, and a minister of the Society of Friends, born at York 22nd Oct., 1825, died at York 31st Aug., 1890; married 7th June, 1855, Mary, only daughter of Isaac Robson, of Dalton, Huddersfield (by Sarah Wheeler, his wife), and had 2 sons and 2 daughters, all born at York:

(1) Mary Louisa Backhouse, born 2nd Sept., 1857.

(2) James Backhouse, of York, practical botanist, born 14th April, 1861; married at Saffron Walden 15th May, 1890, Mabel Grace, daughter of Walter Robson, of Saffron Walden, and has a son:

James Backhouse, born at Harrogate, 15th Aug., 1892.

(3) William Edward Backhouse, born 5th Feb., 1865, died 18th Sept., 1883.

(4) Helen Robson Backhouse, born 25th March, and died 22nd Aug., 1870.

(3) Mary Backhouse, born at York, 18th July, and died 25th August, 1827.

(5) Mary Backhouse, born at Darlington 13th March, 1796, died at Tunbridge Wells 18th Dec., 1824; married at York 20th Sept., 1822, as 1st wife to Richard Janson of London, stockbroker (Foster and Janson, now Foster and Braithwaite); by his 2nd wife, Ann Foster, he had a son Richard; he died at Tottenham 18th July, 1830, aged 32, having had a daughter by his first wife:

Mary Jane Janson, born 9th March, 1824, and died young.

(6) Joseph Backhouse, of Gainford, born at Darlington 19th May, 1798, died at Gainford, 18th Jan., 1881; married 21st April, 1825, Mary Ann, daughter of John Holmes, of Tivetshall Hall, Norfolk; she was born 25th Oct., 1791, and died 28th March, 1874, aged 82, having had 3 daughters:

(1) Mary Matilda Backhouse, born 15th Feb., 1826, died 23rd June, 1828.

(2) Jane Eliza Backhouse, born 28th June, 1827; married at Scarborough 19th Aug., 1862, to William Simpson, of Walton-on-Thames, sometime of Sunderland, Gainford, and Redcar (son of Robert, of Melksham), and has had 4 daughters:

(1) Marion Backhouse Simpson, born 24th May, 1863.

(2) Rosamonde Backhouse Simpson, born 10th May, 1865.

(3) Cicely Elizabeth Backhouse Simpson, born 6th Feb., 1867.

(4) Winifred Matilda Holmes Backhouse Simpson, born 26th May, 1868, died at Ventnor 24th June, 1889.

(3) Mary Backhouse, born at Ravenswood, Michigan, U.S.A., 1834, and died same year.

(7) Elizabeth Backhouse, born at Darlington 9th Feb., 1800, died 3rd December, 1882.

(8) Sarah Backhouse, born at Darlington 7th, and died there 18th Jan., 1802.

(9) Sarah Backhouse, born at Darlington 30th March, 1803, died at York 1st July, 1877.

(10) Ann Dorothy Backhouse, born at Darlington 13th May, 1805, died at York 16th April, 1829.

Joseph Backhouse.
1768-1881.

Mrs. Joseph Backhouse
1791-1874

Elizabeth Backhouse
1800-1882.

Sarah Backhouse
1803-1877

John King
1786-1870.

Mrs. John King
Died, 1874.

John King

Mrs John King
Died, 18[illegible]2.

KING OF MANCHESTER.

WILLIAM BACKHOUSE, of Yealand, removed to Over Kellet about 1727, became a minister of the Society of Friends, and in that capacity visited Iceland and North America; born at Yealand, $169\frac{5}{6}$, i. 13, died at Kellet 1761, v. 21; married at Colthouse, 1720, iv. 21, Agnes, daughter of Richard Atkinson, of Monk Coniston (by his wife Sarah, daughter of Reginald Walker, of Fell Foot, Little Langdale); she was born 1697, xii. 4, and died 8th or 29th Nov., 1773, having had 6 sons and 7 daughters (see page 15): of whom, **(5)** Agnes Backhouse (5th child, and 3rd but only daughter to have issue), born at Kellet 1730, viii. 14, died 25th March, 1797; married at Darlington 1764, ix. 13, to John Harrison, of Darlington (son of Richard and Mary Harrison, of Burton, near Barnsley); he was born 1725, iv. 20, and died at Darlington 29th Jan., 1800, having had, with a son Richard, born and died 1771, 2 daughters, Agnes the younger died 1828, aged 61, and the elder,

Mary Harrison, born at Darlington 17th July, 1765, died at Newcastle-upon-Tyne 28th Jan., 1805; married, 1st, at Darlington 9th May, 1785, to Joseph King, of Newcastle (son of James King and his wife Anne Goldsborough); he died 5th March, 1790, aged 40; she re-married at Darlington 26th Sept., 1804, as 2nd wife to John Richardson, of Sunderland, tanner, who died at Croydon 29th Aug., 1842, aged 77. By her 1st husband Joseph King she had, with one other child that died in infancy, 2 sons and a daughter: (*a*)

(1 *a*) John King, of Manchester, born at Newcastle-upon-Tyne, 2nd June, 1786, died at Greenheys 24th June, 1870; married 16th Oct., 1816, Eleanor, daughter of Samuel Wadkin, of Manchester (by his wife Elizabeth Barrow); she died at Elswick Lodge, Garstang, 1st Nov., 1874, aged 82, having had 6 sons and 4 daughters:

(1) Samuel King, of Elswick Lodge, Garstang, born 11th Sept., 1817.

(2) John King, of Fern Bank, Withington, co. Lanc., and of Manchester, alderman, mayor 1874-5, justice of peace, city of Manchester, 1873, director of London and North Western Railway Company, Nov. 1874-9; born 3rd Nov., 1819; married 5th June, 1856, Frances, daughter of Joseph Fell, of Warrington (by his wife Elizabeth Harrison); she died 4th March, 1892, having had 4 sons and a daughter:

(1) Leonard Goldsborough King, born 21st Sept., 1857.

(2) Alfred John King, B.Sc. London, born 14th Feb., 1859; married 23rd Aug., 1888, Julia Constance, daughter of Thomas and Maria Oliver, of Bollington, Cheshire, and has a daughter:

Ida Mary King, born 11th Oct., 1889.

King, of Mancheste

JOHN BACKHOUSE, of Moss-side near Yealand Redman, co. Lanc., yeoman, died in 1690. See page 13. = SARAH, daug. by his wife in Manserg

A. HANNAH BACKHOUSE, born 1658, died 1729. = JOHN CUMMING, of Hilderstone, mar. 1682, died in 1697. See page 48.

THOMAS BACKHOUSE, of Yealand Redman, born 1661, died 1729. = ALICE, daughter of RICHARD BECKE, of Wythmore in Westmorland, mar. 1696, died 1700. See page 13.

SARAH HOUSE, 1664, ma died 16 wife.

NATHAN HUBBERSTIE = MARY, daughter of Thomas Thornton, of Caton, co. Lanc. (1st wife), mar. 1715, died 1716. = JOHN BACKHOUSE, of Hornby, born 1693, died 1739. See page 14. = MARGARET (2n daughter of JOHN Ayrey, of Ker about 1695, mar. 1772. See page 14.

JAMES BACKHOUSE, of West Lodge, Darlington, flax-dresser and linen manufacturer, established the bank at Darlington 1774, born 1721, died 1798. See page 17. = JANE, only child of JONATHAN HEDLEY, of Darlington, born 1718, mar. at Stockton 1746, died in 1805.

WILLIAM BACKHOUSE, born 1724, sometime of New York, died there 1792, mar. ELIZABETH, daughter of JONATHAN THORNTON, of Caton. She died 1750. See page 16.

B. AGNES 1730, ma

JOSEPH KING, of Newcastle-upon-Tyne (1st husband), m. 9th May, 1785, d. 5th March, 1796, aged 40. = MARY HARRISON, b. at 17th July, 1765, d. 28th See page 39.

JOHN KING, of Manchester, b. 2nd June, 1786, d. 24th June, 1870. See page 39. = ELEANOR, dau. of SAMUEL WADKIN, of Manchester, m. 1816, d. 1st Nov., 1874.

JOSEPH KING, of York, b. 31st Oct., 1787, d. 22nd Nov., 1839. See page 41. = SARAH, da AWMACK, 1810, d. 2n

SAMUEL KING, b. 1817.
JOHN KING, of Manchester, b. 1819, m. 1856, FRANCES, dau. of JOSEPH FELL, of Warrington, she died 1892. See page 39.

MARY KING, b. 1823.
ELEANOR KING, b. 1821, d. 1858, m. 1857, THOMAS CARRICK, of Manchester (2nd wife).

JOSEPH H. KING, b. 1827, m. 1853, SARAH, dau. of JOHN ROOKE, of Manchester. See page 41.

THOMAS B. KING, b. 1832, m. 1860, MARGARET ROOKE, who d. 1868.

WILLIAM KING, b. 1835, m. 1867, ANN, dau. of JOSH. FELL.

JAMES m. 1864 GARET dau. of SIMPS Manch

LEONARD G. KING, b. 1857.
ALFRED JOHN KING, b. 1850, m. 1878, JULIA C. OLIVER.
IDA MARY KING, b. 1889.

ELIZABETH F. KING.
GEORGE KING, born 1863.
HAROLD KING, born 1867.

JOHN ARTHUR CARRICK, born 1858, m. 1882, CHARLOTTE E. ROBERTSON.

ELEANOR KING, m. 1886, to CHARLES JAMES LILWALL.
GLADYS MARGARET LILWALL, born 1889.
MARY ELEANOR, born 1891.

FREDERICK ROOKE K., b. 1866.

ROBERT W. KING.
MARY D. KING.

GEORGE S. KING.
SARAH H. KING.
JAMES E. KING.

HENRY KING
1821.
See Page 42.

MARY J. KING

WILLIAM S. KING.
See Page 42.

HENRIETTA KING.

(3) Elizabeth Fell King, born 1st Jan., 1861.
(4) George King, born 31st Oct., 1863.
(5) Harold King, born 23rd March, 1867.

(3) Eleanor King, born 12th Sept., 1821, died 15th June, 1858; married 28th May, 1857, as 2nd wife to Thomas Carrick, of Manchester, who died 27th May, 1873, leaving by her a son:

John Arthur Carrick, of Southport, born 4th June, 1858; married 7th June, 1882, Charlotte Elizabeth, daughter of Charles Augustus Hook Robertson, of Bristol.

(4) Mary King, born 20th Aug., 1823.

(5) Elizabeth King, born 20th Oct., 1824, died unmarried 28th Jan., 1879.

(6) Joseph Harrison King, born 18th Dec., 1827; married 22nd Sept., 1853, Sarah, daughter of John and Mary Rooke, of Manchester, *s.p.*

(7) Ann King, born 28th April, 1830, died 28th June following.

(8) Thomas Barrow King, born 22nd June, 1832; married 5th April, 1860, Margaret, daughter of John and Mary Rooke aforesaid, she died 6th May, 1868, having had 2 sons and a daughter:

(1) Eleanor King, born 26th June, 1861, married 5th Aug., 1886, to Charles James Lilwall, of Hay, co. Hereford, and has 2 daughters:
(1) Gladys Margaret Lilwall, born 26th Feb., 1889.
(2) Mary Eleanor Lilwall, born 2nd Oct., 1891.
(2) Ernest Wadkin King, born May, 1864, died 24th Jan., 1865.
(3) Frederick Rooke King, born 23rd Feb., 1866.

(9) William King (twin with James), born 31st Jan., 1835; married 10th Oct., 1867, Ann, daughter of Joseph Fell aforesaid, and has had a son and 2 daughters:

(1) Annie Mabel King, born 29th March, 1869, died 31st May following.
(2) Robert William King, B.Sc. London, born 15th June, 1870.
(3) Mary Dorothea King, born 19th April, 1873.

(10) James King (twin with William), born 31st Jan., 1835; married 25th Feb., 1864, Margaret Harrison, daughter of George and Sarah Simpson, of Manchester, and has had 3 sons and a daughter:

(1) George Simpson King, born 3rd May, 1865.
(2) John King, born 20th May, 1867, died 9th April, 1875.
(3) Sarah Harrison King, born 21st March, 1869.
(4) James Edward King, born 11th Oct., 1872.

(2*a*) Joseph King, Newcastle-upon-Tyne, and afterwards of York, born 31st Oct., 1787, died there 22nd Nov., 1839; married 13th Nov., 1810, Sarah, daughter of Joseph Awmack, of York; she died there 2nd Dec., 1855, aged 70, having had 6 sons and 2 daughters:

(1) John King, born at York 12th Oct., 1811, died there 8th Feb., 1823.

(2) Joseph King, born at York 13th Aug., 1813, died there 10th July, 1821.
(3) James Harrison King, of York, born there 14th Jan., 1817, died *s.p.* 7th Oct., 1855; married 16th July, 1846, Hannah, daughter of William Benson, of Stang End, lastly of Ulverston; she died at York, 24th March, 1892, having re-married 14th April, 1859, to William Brady, of York, who died 20th Sept. following.
(4) Mary King, born at York 10th Sept., 1818, died there 10th Dec., 1821.
(5) William King, born at York 24th Dec., 1819, died there 3rd March, 1821.
(6) Henry King, of York, born there 23rd Oct., 1821; married 1st at Malton 21st Feb., 1850, Esther Richardson, daughter of Abraham Sewell, of Malton; she died at Birkenhead, 13th Nov., 1853, aged 28, leaving a son and 2 daughters:

(1) Mary Jane King, born 28th Nov., 1850.
(2) William Sewell King, born 25th July, 1852; married 18th Sept., 1878, Kate Harris, daughter of Thomas Hudswell, of Leeds, and has had 3 sons and 1 daughter:

(1) Herbert Hudswell King, born 19th Aug., 1880, died 23rd Sept. following.
(2) Henry Foster King, born 5th Aug., 1885.
(3) Harold Awmack King, born 19th July, 1887.
(4) Ethel Dorothy King, born 21st March, 1892.

(3) Henrietta King, born 27th Oct., 1853.

Henry King married 2ndly, 5th Jan., 1860, Sarah, daughter of Henry Casson, of Hull; she died at York 19th June, 1866, aged 32, leaving a son and 3 daughters:

(4) Agnes Harrison King, born 13th Nov., 1860; married 10th June, 1885, to Joseph Taylor Sewell, of Whitby, and has 2 sons and a daughter:

(1) Arnold Edward Sewell, born 21st June, 1886.
(2) Agnes Margaret Sewell, born 12th April, 1888.
(3) Joseph King Sewell, born 7th June, 1890.

(5) Henry King, of Bundarra, Glenrowan, Victoria, born 24th Oct., 1862; married 16th Dec., 1891, Ada Macfarlane, of Ardchattan, Victoria, and has a daughter:—Sarah Elizabeth King, born 26th Sept., 1892.
(6) Esther Richardson King, born 8th Feb., 1864; married 4th June, 1890, to Charles Binks, of York, and has a son and daughter:

(1) Harold Binks, born 16th April, 1891.
(2) Winifred Binks, born 1 Sept., 1892.

(7) Emily King, born 12th Jan., 1865; married 3rd June, 1891, to Henry John Lloyd, of York, and has a son:—Eric Lloyd, born 19th March, 1892.

(7) Edward King, born at York 5th Dec., 1822, died there 23rd Nov., 1869.
(8) Sarah Ann King, born at York 24th Nov., 1829, died 13th March, 1831.

Myles B. Foster.
1783-1861
See Page 43.

Mrs M. B. Foster
1790-1884

Myles B. Foster
See Page 46.

Robert Foster
See Page 43

Mrs Robert Foster
1823-1893.

JOSEPH FOSTER
1813-1892.

MRS JOSEPH FOSTER
1811-1898.

SANDYS B. FOSTER

MRS W. H. RICHARDSON

JOSEPH FOSTER

(3 *a*) Child born and died in 1788.

(4 *a*) Ann King (only daughter of Joseph King and Mary Harrison, see page 39), born at Newcastle-upon-Tyne 29th Sept., 1790, died in London 28th November, 1884; married at Newcastle 11th April, 1811, to Myles Birket Foster, then of North Shields, and afterwards of London, (son of Robert Foster, of Hebblethwaite Hall, Yorks, sometime lieutenant in the Navy); he died in London 21st Jan., 1861, aged 76, having had 6 sons and a daughter :

(1) Robert Foster, of Newcastle-upon-Tyne, born at North Shields 27th Jan., 1812; married 7th July, 1858, Ann, only surviving daughter of Isaac Richardson, of Newcastle-upon-Tyne (and his wife Deborah, daughter of David Sutton); she died 10th July, 1893.

(2) Joseph Foster, of Sunderland, born at North Shields 19th Aug., 1813, died at Sunderland 9th Feb., 1859; married at North Shields 19th July, 1842, Elizabeth, 4th daughter of Emmanuel Taylor, shipowner of that place, she died 22nd Dec., 1888, aged 77, having had 5 sons and 3 daughters :

(1) Annie Foster, born at Sunderland 23rd Feb., 1843; married in London, 20th Sept., 1881, as 2nd wife to William Henry Richardson, alderman and J.P., co. Durham, born 1829.

(2) Joseph Foster, Hon. M.A. Oxon., author of "Alumni Oxonienses," "The British Peerage," &c.; for an account of his principal genealogical works see "Men and Women of the Time"; born in Sunderland 9th March, 1844; married at Burgess Hill, Sussex, 12th Aug., 1869, Catherine Clarke, eldest daughter of late George Pocock, of that place, and has 2 sons and 3 daughters :

(1) Sandys Birket Foster, Associate of the Institute of Chartered Accountants, 1892, born at New Barnet, Herts, 19th June, 1870.

(2) Maude Katharine Foster, born in London 7th Oct., 1873.

(3) Esmay Alice Foster, born in London 27th March, 1877.

(4) Evelyn Mary Foster, born in London 12th March, 1881.

(5) Josslyn Foster, born in London 28th Dec., 1882.

(3) James Foster, born at Sunderland, 2nd Oct., 1845; married at Newcastle-upon-Tyne 13th Nov., 1866, Theodosia Alice, elder daughter of Alexander Milne, of Aberdeen, sometime of Sunderland; she died at Twynning, co. Gloucester, 29th March, 1884. He married 2ndly, at Sunderland, 12th March, 1885, Elizabeth, widow of James Fairman, of Sunderland, 3rd daughter of late Robert Ferry, of the same place. By his 1st wife he has a son and daughter, both born in Sunderland :

(1) Theodosia Alice Foster, born 1st Feb., 1868.

(2) Myles Birket Foster, born 30th March, 1875.

ed there
Browne.
born at
born at

nd Redmayne,
rr, of Ridgend,

NET, = JOHN
lter of ROBINSON,
GOD- of Yealand,
E, of Yea- mar. 1701,
Conyers, 2nd hus-
1691. band.

=AGNES, daughter of RICHARD, ATKINSON, of Monk Coniston, born in 1697, mar. in 1720, died in 1773.

3rd June,
5th April,
she died

HN BACKHOUSE, of Lancaster, born
33, died in New York 1775, mar.
57 JANE, daughter of GEORGE DODG-
N, of Kendal, she died 1763.

See page 16.

Sunderland, tanner, mar. (his
804, died 29th Aug., 1842.

essbrook,
, 1881, as
ere :

LES BIRKET FOSTER, of North
elds, afterwards of London, where
died 21st Jan., 1861.

1. ROBERT FOS of Newcastl), Tyne, born 1814 te of ,

5. MARY, born 1821, mar. 1852, to WILLIAM ATCHISON, of London.

ANN (1st wife), 10th dau. of ROBERT SPENCE, of North Shields, mar. 1850, died 1859. = 6. MYLES BIRKET FOSTER, of Witley, Surrey, born 1825. = FRANCES (2nd wife), dau. of DAWSON WATSON, of Sedbergh, Yorks, mar. 1864.

nmarried.
5th Dec.,
4th and
sons and

ANNIE FOSTER, mar. 1881, to W. H. RICHARDSON, now of Milford, Surrey.

JO 18 C.

DORY FLORENCE born 1860, 1887, to REV. N WADDELL CK.

MYLES BIRKET FOSTER, born 1851, mar. 1881, CHRISTINE LORIMER.

WILLIAM FOSTER. HENRY FOSTER, of Newcastle-on-Tyne, born 1854, mar. 1883, ETHEL CLAPHAM.

MARGARET ANN F., born 1856, mar. 1st, 1881, to JOHN H. DALE, who died 1892, remarried, 1893, to H. E. A. STADNITSKI.

ELLEN FOSTER, born 1857, mar. 1886, to LANCELOT T. GLASSON.

ec., 1889.

died 30th
Rutty, of
daughter,

SANDYS BIRKET FOSTER, born 1870.
MAUDE K., born 1873.
ESMAY A., born 1877.
EVELYN M., born 1881
JOSSLYN, born 1882.

OSTER B., died 1893.

MYLES BIRKET, born 1884.
DOROTHY M., born 1885.
JOHN L., born 1886.

MABEL C., born 1888.
ROBERT S., born 1891.
ARTHUR E., born 1893.

HENRY C. F.
DOROTHY.
MARY.

MARGARET E. GLASSON.

Foster, formerly of co. Durham.

JOHN BACKHOUSE, of Moss-side near Yealand Redman, co. Lanc., yeoman, died in 1690. See page 13. = SARAH, daughter of William Jackson, of Yealand Redmayne, by his wife Mabel, heiress of her brother John Carr, of Ridgend, in Mansergh, born about 1626, died 1706.

A

HANNAH BACKHOUSE, born 1658, died 1729. = JOHN CUMMING, of Hilderstone, mar. 1682, died in 1697. See page 48.

THOMAS BACKHOUSE, of Yealand Redman, born 1661, died 1729. = ALICE, daughter of RICHARD BECKE, of Wythmore in Westmorland, mar. 1696, died 1700. See page 13.

SARAH BACKHOUSE, born 1664, mar. 1688, died 1697, 1st wife. = GEORGE ROBINSON, of Yealand Conyers, died 1719. See page 14.

JAMES BACKHOUSE, of Yealand Conyers, born 1668, died in Lancaster Castle, 1697 (1st husband). See page 14. = JANET, daughter of JOHN GODSALVE, of Yealand Conyers, mar. 1691. = JOHN ROBINSON, of Yealand, mar. 1701, 2nd husband.

B

NATHAN HUBBERSTIE = MARY, daughter of THOMAS THORNTON, of Caton, co. Lanc. (1st wife), mar. 1715, died 1716. See page 14. = JOHN BACKHOUSE, of Hornby, born 1693, died 1739. See page 14. = MARGARET (2nd wife), daughter of JOHN and RUTH AYREY, of Kendal, born about 1695, mar. 1720, died 1772.

WILLIAM BACKHOUSE, of Yealand, a minister of the Society of Friends, born 1696, died 1761. See page 15. = AGNES, daughter of RICHARD ATKINSON, of Monk Coniston, born in 1697, mar. in 1720, died in 1773.

C

JAMES BACKHOUSE, of West Lodge, Darlington, flax-dresser and linen manufacturer, established the bank at Darlington 1774, born 1721, died 1798. See page 17. = JANE, only child of JONATHAN HEDLEY, of Darlington, born 1718, mar. at Stockton 1746, died in 1805.

WILLIAM BACKHOUSE, born 1724, sometime of New York, died there 1792, mar. ELIZABETH, daughter of JONATHAN THORNTON, of Caton. She died 1750. See page 16.

AGNES BACKHOUSE, born 1730, mar. 1764, died 1797. = JOHN HARRISON, of Darlington, born 1725, died 1800.

JOHN BACKHOUSE, of Lancaster, born 1733, died in New York 1775, mar. 1757 JANE, daughter of GEORGE DODGSON, of Kendal, she died 1763. See page 16.

JOSEPH KING, of Newcastle-upon-Tyne (1st husband), mar. 9th May, 1785, died 5th March, 1796, aged 40. = MARY HARRISON, born at Darlington 17th July, 1765, died 28th Jan., 1805. See page 39. = JOHN RICHARDSON, of Sunderland, tanner, mar. (his 2nd wife) 26th Sept., 1804, died 29th Aug., 1842.

D

JOHN KING, of Manchester, born 2nd June, 1786, died 24th June, 1870. = ELEANOR, dau. of SAMUEL WADKIN, of Manchester, mar. 1816, died 1st Nov., 1874. See page 39.

JOSEPH KING, of York, born 31st Oct., 1787, died 22nd Nov., 1839. See page 41. = SARAH, dau. of JOSEPH AWMACK, of York, mar. 1810, died 2nd Dec., 1855.

ANN KING, born 29th Sept., 1790, mar. 11th April, 1811, died 28th Nov., 1884. See page 43. = MYLES BIRKET FOSTER, of North Shields, afterwards of London, where he died 21st Jan., 1861.

E

1. ROBERT FOSTER, of Newcastle-on-Tyne, born 1812. = ANN, dau. of ISAAC RICHARDSON, of Newcastle, mar. 1858, died 1893.

2. JOSEPH FOSTER, of Sunderland, born 1813, died 1859. See page 43. = ELIZABETH, 4th dau. of E. TAYLOR, of N. Shields, died 1888.

3. DODSHON FOSTER, of London, born 1816, died 1876. = MARY ANN, dau. of JOHN RUTTY, of London, mar. 1849, died 1876.

MARY HESLETINE (1st wife), dau. of G. P. HOWES, of London, mar. 1849, died 1852. = 4. JOHN HARRISON FOSTER, of Witley, Surrey, born 1818. = JULIANA (2nd wife), 2nd dau. of late CHARLES ODLIN, of Stamford, co. Linc., mar. 1883.

5. MARY, born 1821, mar. 1852, to WILLIAM ATCHISON, of London.

ANN (1st wife), 10th dau. of ROBERT SPENCE, of North Shields, mar. 1850, died 1859. = 6. MYLES BIRKET FOSTER, of Witley, Surrey, born 1825. = FRANCES (2nd wife), dau. of DAWSON WATSON, of Sedbergh, Yorks, mar. 1864.

Children of Robert Foster:
- ANNIE FOSTER, mar. 1881, to W. H. RICHARDSON, now of Milford, Surrey.

Children of Joseph Foster:
- JOSEPH FOSTER, born 1844, mar. 1869, CATHERINE C. POCOCK.
  - SANDYS BIRKET FOSTER, born 1870. MAUDE E., born 1873. EDWAY A., born 1877. EVELYN M., born 1881. JOSELYN, born 1882.
- JAMES FOSTER, born 1845, mar. 1st, ALICE MILNE, who died 1884 (and 2ndly, ELIZABETH FAIRMAN).
  - ALICE T. FOSTER, born 1868. MYLES B., born 1875.
- ELIZABETH, mar. 1873, to JOHN L. BROWNE, of Sunderland.
  - LUCY F. BROWNE. HAROLD M. JESSIE F. ARTHUR L. LINDSAY F. JOHN CORBET. LEONARD S.
- ROBERT, of Sunderland, died 1890, mar. 1873, ANNE H. FERRY, who died 1893.
  - WINIFRED. MURIEL. HILDA.
- AGNES FOSTER, died 1888, mar. 1881 to JAMES BOWES, of Bessbrook, co. Armagh.
  - SYDNEY F. BOWES. GEOFFREY F. FRANK F.
- EMMANUEL T. FOSTER.
- FREDERICK FOSTER, of Sunderland, born 1853, mar. 1879, EMILY JANE FERRY.
  - ELSIE FOSTER. FREDERICK. EDITH. JOHN M.
- JESSIE FOSTER, mar. 1872, to Frederick B. Shuttleworth.
- EDWIN FOSTER.
- CHARLES FOSTER, born 1854, died 1890, mar. 1876, ISABELLA, dau. of J. M. BUCKHAM, of Whitehaven.
  - CYRIL DODSHON FOSTER, born 1878. MARY GERTRUDE. ALICE JESSIE.

Children of John Harrison Foster:
- ALICE MARY.
- FANNY ISABEL FOSTER, mar. 1887. = EDWARD SHEARBURN MARSHALL, M.A., Vicar of Milford, Surrey.
  - EDWARD FOSTER M., born 1888. PHYLLIS MARY. GERTRUDE ISOBEL. JOHN WORDSWORTH M., born and died 1893.

Children of Mary and William Atchison:
- THOMAS PERCY A., born 1857, mar. 1882, MARY REYNOLDS.
  - ETHEL MARGARETTE A. CHARLES FOSTER A. HAROLD PERCY A.
- MARY FLORENCE A., born 1860, mar. 1887, to REV. JOHN WADDELL BLACK.
  - JOHN FOSTER B., born 1889, died 1893.

Children of Myles Birket Foster:
- MYLES BIRKET FOSTER, born 1851, mar. 1881, CHRISTINE LORIMER.
  - MYLES BIRKET, born 1884. DOROTHY M., born 1885. JOHN L., born 1886.
- WILLIAM FOSTER.
- HENRY FOSTER, of Newcastle-on-Tyne, born 1854, mar. 1883, ETHEL CLAPHAM.
  - MABEL C., born 1888. ROBERT S., born 1891. ARTHUR E., born 1893. HENRY C. F. DOROTHY. MARY.
- MARGARET ANN F., born 1856, mar. 1st, 1881, to JOHN H. DALE, who died 1892, remarried, 1893, to H. E. A. STADNITSKI.
- ELLEN FOSTER, born 1857, mar. 1886, to LANCELOT T. GLASSON.
  - MARGARET E. GLASSON.

(4) Elizabeth Foster, born at Sunderland 15th Nov., 1846; married there 13th March, 1873, to John Laing Browne, 3rd son of late Joseph Browne, of Newcastle-upon-Tyne, and his wife Margaret Laing; he was born at Newcastle 26th Sept., 1842, and has 5 sons and 2 daughters, all born at Sunderland:

(1) Lucy Foster Browne, born 31st March, 1875.
(2) Harold Montagu Browne, born 15th Sept., 1877.
(3) Jessie Foster Browne, born 29th Oct., 1879.
(4) Arthur Laing Browne, born 9th July, 1881.
(5) Lindsay Foster Browne, born 29th May, 1883.
(6) John Corbet Browne, born 17th Feb., 1885.
(7) Leonard Southaicke Browne, born 22nd May, 1887.

(5) Robert Foster, of Sunderland, town councillor, born there 23rd June, 1848, died in London, 28th March, 1890; married at Sunderland 16th April, 1873, Anne Hides, eldest daughter of late Robert Ferry aforesaid, she died 2nd May, 1893, leaving 3 daughters, all born at Sunderland:

(1) Annie Winifred Foster, born 30th April, 1874.
(2) Muriel Foster, twin with
(3) Hilda Foster, born 22nd Nov., 1877.

(6) Agnes Foster, born at North Shields 28th Sept., 1850, died at Bessbrook, co. Armagh, 28th March, 1888; married at Sunderland 24th Feb., 1881, as 1st wife to James Bowes, of Bessbrook, and had 3 sons, all born there:

(1) Sydney Foster Bowes, born 1st Dec., 1881.
(2) Geoffrey Foster Bowes, born 28th Sept., 1885.
(3) Frank Foster Bowes, born 19th Feb., 1888.

(7) Emanuel Taylor Foster, born at North Shields 2nd June, 1852; unmarried.

(8) Frederick Foster, of Sunderland, born at North Shields 16th Dec., 1853; married at Sunderland 16th April, 1879, Emily Jane, 4th and youngest daughter of late Robert Ferry aforesaid, and has had 3 sons and 2 daughters, all born at Sunderland:

(1) Elsie Foster, born 16th March, 1880.
(2) Frederick Foster, born 3rd Sept., 1881.
(3) Edith Foster, born 31st March, 1883.
(4) Robert Foster Foster, born 27th Nov., 1885, died 25th Dec., 1889.
(5) John Maurice Foster, born 2nd Dec., 1889.

(3) Dodshon Foster, of London, born at North Shields 6th Jan., 1816, died 30th March, 1876; married 6th Feb., 1849, Mary Ann, daughter of John Rutty, of Paddington; she died 5th Aug., 1876, aged 57, leaving 2 sons and a daughter, all born in London:

Robert Foster
See Page 43

Joseph Foster
1813-1859
See Page 43

Birket Foster
See Page 46

Dodshon Foster
1816-1876
See Page 44

John H. Foster
See Page 45

(1) Jessie Foster, born 2nd Feb., 1851; married in London, 6th Feb., 1872, to Frederick Brandon, 2nd son of late William Sewell Shuttleworth, of Plaistow Hall, Kent.

(2) Edwin Foster, born 27th Aug., 1852.

(3) Charles Foster, born 26th Aug., 1854, died in New York 13th Dec., 1890; married 13th Dec., 1876, Isabella, daughter of Joseph Milward Buckham, of Whitehaven, and had a son and 2 daughters:

(1) Cyril Dodshon Foster, born at Barnet, Herts, 8th May, 1878.

(2) Mary Gertrude Foster, born at Witley, 11th Feb., 1882.

(3) Alice Jessie Foster, born at Thursley, Surrey, 22nd June, 1886.

(4) John Harrison Foster, of Fernside, Witley, Surrey, born at North Shields, 22nd Jan., 1818; married 1st, 24th May, 1849, Mary Hesletine, daughter of George Pigott Howes, of London; she died 11th Aug., 1882. He married 2ndly, 18th Oct., 1883, Juliana, 2nd daughter of late Charles Odlin, of Stamford, co. Lincoln. By his 1st wife he had a son and 4 daughters, all born in London:

(1) Edith Foster, born 17th Dec., 1852, died 14th July, 1877.

(2) Alice Mary Foster, born 4th April, 1854.

(3) Amy Gertrude Foster, born 27th June, 1855, died 20th Aug., 1859.

(4) Fanny Isabel Foster, born 17th Oct., 1857; married at Witley, 16th August, 1887, to Rev. Edward Shearburn Marshall, M.A. Brasenose College, Oxford, Vicar of Milford, Surrey, 1890, and has had 2 sons and 2 daughters:

(1) Edward Foster Marshall, born at Witley, 2nd Aug., 1888.

(2) Phyllis Mary Marshall, born at Witley, 5th Aug., 1889.

(3) Gertrude Isobel Marshall, born at Milford, 12th Nov., 1890.

(4) John Wordsworth Marshall, born at Milford, 28th May, 1893, died 14th August following.

(5) Walter John Foster, born 12th Aug., 1860, died 25th Oct., 1885.

(5) Mary Foster, born at North Shields 19th Nov., 1821; married 22nd June, 1852, to William Atchison, of London, and has had 2 sons and 2 daughters, all born there:

(1) Mary Catherine Atchison, born 23rd May, 1853, died 21st March, 1854.

(2) William Ernest Atchison, born 2nd August, 1854, died unmarried 18th Nov., 1889.

(3) Thomas Percy Atchison, born 28th July, 1857; married 1st June, 1882, Mary, daughter of Charles Reynolds, of London, and has 2 sons and a daughter:

(1) Ethel Margarette Atchison, born 12th May, 1883.

(2) Charles Foster Atchison, born 22nd Sept., 1885.

(3) Harold Percy Reynolds Atchison, born 21st March, 1889.

(4) Mary Florence Atchison, born 23rd Aug., 1860; married 15th June, 1887, to Rev. John Waddell Black, and had a son:

(1) John Foster Black, born in London, 29th April, 1889, died at Port Stanley, Ontario, 12th March, 1893.

(6) Myles Birket Foster, of The Hill, Witley, Surrey, a member of the Royal Water-colour Society (see "Men and Women of the Time" and Virtue's "Art Annual," 1890), born at North Shields 4th Feb., 1825; married 1st at Earsdon, Northumberland, 13th Aug., 1850, his cousin Ann, 10th daughter of Robert Spence, of North Shields; she died 4th July, 1859, aged 34. He married 2ndly, 25th Aug., 1864, Frances, daughter of Dawson Watson, of Sedbergh, Yorks. By his 1st wife he had 3 sons and 2 daughters, all born in London:

(1) Myles Birket Foster, Associate Royal Academy of Music, &c. (see Brown's "Dictionary of Musicians"), born 29th Nov., 1851; married in Edinburgh 6th Jan., 1881, Christine, daughter of James Lorimer, C.E., and has 4 sons and 2 daughters, all born at Willesden:

(1) Myles Birket Foster, born 22nd Aug., 1884.

(2) Dorothy Margaret Foster, born 9th October, 1885.

(3) John Lorimer Foster, born 15th October, 1886.

(4) Mabel Christine Foster, born 24th Jan., 1888.

(5) Robert Spence Foster, born 11th June, 1891.

(6) Arthur Edward Foster, born 17th June, 1893.

(2) William Foster, born 6th June, 1853; unmarried.

(3) Henry Foster, of Newcastle-upon-Tyne, born 6th Nov., 1854; married 26th July, 1883, his second cousin Ethel, eldest daughter of late Henry Clapham, of Newcastle-upon-Tyne, and has a son and 2 daughters:

(1) Henry Clapham Foster, born at Backworth, Northumberland, 27th May, 1885.

(2) Dorothy Foster, born at Backworth, 2nd June, 1889.

(3) Mary Foster, born at Newcastle, 14th July, 1892.

(4) Margaret Ann Foster, born 27th Jan., 1856; married 1st at Witley, 25th Aug., 1881, to John Henry, eldest son of John Brodrick Dale, of Westoe, co. Durham, and of South Shields, banker; he died *s.p.* 26th Feb., 1892, and she re-married at Witley, 18th July, 1893, to Henri Etienne Adrien Stadnitski, of Amsterdam and Geneva.

(5) Ellen Foster, born 24th Sept., 1857; married 22nd Dec., 1886, to Lancelot Thompson Glasson, of Lincoln's Inn, barrister-at-law (3rd son of late Thomas Glasson, of Penrith), and has a daughter:

(1) Margaret Ellen Glasson, born at Sevenoaks, 28th Dec., 1891.

(7) James Foster, born in London 14th Nov., 1830, died there 22nd April, 1832.

PER · SE · VERE

PEARSON OF POOLBANK,

WESTMORLAND.

HANNAH BACKHOUSE (eldest daughter of John Backhouse, of Moss Side, near Yealand Redmayne, co. Lanc., see page 13), born at Yealand Redmayne 1658, viii. 28, and died at Hilderstone 1729, iv. 8; married 1682, iii. 24, to John (son of Edward) Cumming, of Hilderstone; he died there 1697, xi. 28, having had 2 sons and 3 daughters: (*a*)

(1 *a*) Edward Cumming, born 1684, ix. 30, buried at Hilderstone 1684, x. 6.

(2 *a*) Ann Cumming, born 1686, ii. 27, died 1722, viii. 18; married at Yealand 1717, ix. 7, as 1st wife to John Lancaster, of Wray, and sometime of Burton, and had a son and daughter:

(1) Hannah Lancaster, born 1718, vi. 17, died at Burton 1739, xii. 4.

(2) James Lancaster, born 1719-20, i. 18, died 1721, iii. 5.

(3 *a*) Edward Cumming, of Hilderstone, born 1688, i. 25, died there 1771, ii. 6, aged 82 years and 10 months; he married 1720, viii. 27, Ann, daughter of Richard Sill, of Birkrigg Park in Preston Richard, she died at Hilderstone 1761, vi. 24, aged 64, having had 2 sons and a daughter:

(1) Hannah Cumming, died 1771, v. 3; married at Yealand Conyers 1740, viii. 22, to Thomas Pearson, of Poolbank, Westmorland, yeoman (son of Joseph, of Fellside), [who

---

(2) John Cumming, born 1723, vi. 18, died next day.

(3) John Cumming, of Hilderstone, yeoman, born there 1724, vi. 28, and died there 1st May, 1801, aged 76; devisee under the wills of John Backhouse, 1763, and of Richard Backhouse, 1764 (see pages 81, 82); married at Height in Cartmel, 1763, xii. 27, Hannah, daughter of William Salthouse, of Ulverston, ironmonger; she died 16th Nov., 1809, aged 72, having had at least 2 sons and a daughter:

(1) Edward Cumming, of Hilderstone, born 1765, vi. 18, died *s.p.*

(2) Hannah Cumming, born 1768, iii. 20, died at Kendal 18th Sept., 1842, aged 74; married at Yealand 4th Jan., 1804, to her 3rd cousin, George Backhouse, of Kendal, ironmonger and stamp distributor. He died 23rd Oct., 1830, having had a son and daughter (see p. 16):

(3) John Backhouse Cumming, born 1770, vi. 21, and died 1784, v. 4.

(4 *a*) SARAH CUMMING, married to Thomas Beakbane, of whom see page 57.

(5 *a*) Mary Cumming, born 1692, iii. 13, died 1705.

who died (perhaps) 1771, v. 31, having had at least 2 sons and 4 daughters : (*b*)·

(1 *b*) Joseph Pearson, born 1742, viii. 27, died 1745, v. 17.

(2 *b*) Ann Pearson, died unmarried.

(3 *b*) Hannah Pearson, born 1748, xii. 23, died 25th July, 1819.

(4 *b*) Agnes Pearson, born 1749, viii. 11, died 19th Aug., 1829, aged 80; married at Preston Patrick 1781, vi. 4, to John Albright, of Lancaster, sail canvas maker (son of Thomas and Mary, of Lancaster); died 24th March, 1830, aged 84, having had a son and 6 daughters : (*c*)

(1 *c*) Thomas Albright, of Lancaster, sail cloth manufacturer, and of Newland House, Scotforth, yeoman, emigrated to the United States, born at Lancaster 1782, iii. 30, died at Hannibal, Missouri, 20th March, 1848, aged 66; he married Sarah, daughter of Joseph Whitlark, of Nottingham; she died at Hannibal, Marion Co., U.S.A., 26th Sept., 1844, aged 57, having had (with 3 children who died very young) 12 sons and 4 daughters, all born at Lancaster:

(1) John Albright, of Lancaster, born 13th Aug., 1811, died 19th July 1887; married at Lancaster 1835, Margaret, daughter of John Dodd, of Dent, Yorks, she died 19th Aug., 1863, having had 2 sons and 2 daughters, all born at Lancaster:

(1) Mary Albright, born at Lancaster 3rd Sept., 1836; married, 1st, to Thomas Brewer, and had a son, Frederick Brewer; she remarried to Daniel Gudgeon, of Hest Bank, near Lancaster.

(2) Thomas Albright, of Ulverston, born 21st Dec., 1839; married

(3) Charles Albright, of Lancaster, born 29th Dec., 1841; married 18th Sept., 1877, Esther, daughter of John Peel, of Bromfield, Cumberland, *s.p.*

(4) Sarah Albright, born 3rd June, 1844; married 9th Sept., 1873, to John Wells, of Lancaster, and has 2 sons and a daughter, all born there.

(1) John Henry Wells, born 16th Aug., 1874.

(2) Agnes Wells, born 27th Feb., 1876.

(3) Bernard Wells, born 14th July, 1878.

(2) Thomas Albright, of Lancaster, born 24th Dec., 1812; married at Manchester 18th Feb., 1841, Alice, daughter of William Satterthwaite, of Hulme, farmer, and had 2 sons and 7 daughters:

(1) Sarah Alice Albright, born 14th Feb., 1842, died 16th Jan., 1844.

(2) Thomas Albright, born 19th Sept., 1843.

(3) Maria Albright, born 19th July, 1845; married 1888, to William Airey, of St. Michael's, near Liverpool, *s.p.*
(4) Mary Ann Albright, born 3rd Feb., 1847.
(5) Esther Albright, born 5th Dec., 1848; married Aug., 1888, to Harry Evans, of Lancaster, *s.p.*
(6) Emma Albright, born 29th Nov., 1850.
(7) William Albright, born 25th June, 1852.
(8) Agnes Albright, born 29th Nov., 1854.
(9) Rachel Albright, born 26th Nov., 1856.

(3) Henry Albright, of Bootle, Cheshire, chemist and druggist, born 27th July, 1814; married at Preston 23rd Jan., 1845, Rebecca, daughter of Joseph and Rebecca Drewry, of that place; she died 30th May, 1866, aged 45, having had 6 sons and 5 daughters:

(1) Henry Albright, born 20th April, 1846, died unmarried 14th Dec., 1890.
(2) Joseph Drewry Albright, of Birkenhead, born 3rd May, 1848; married and has 2 daughters.
(3) Alfred Albright, born at Liscard 2nd July, 1850.
(4) Sarah Rebecca Albright, born at New Brighton 3rd June, 1852; married to Joseph Poole, of Ferns, co. Wexford.
(5) William Drewry Albright, of Port Mackay, Queensland, born 17th June, 1854.
(6) Anne Albright, a twin with
(7) Edith Albright, born 22nd Feb., 1856, and died 23rd Sept., 1864.
(8) Samuel George Albright, of Fleetwood, born at Newtown, co. Waterford, 15th April, 1858.
(9) Mary Alice Albright, born 25th Aug., 1860, died 20th Dec., 1866.
(10) John Albright, born at Bootle, 17th May, 1862, died 19th Sept., 1864.
(11) Helen Albright, born 22nd April, 1866, died

(4) Joseph Albright, of The Greaves, Lancaster, born 23rd Jan., 1816; married 1st at Bolton-le-Sands, near Lancaster, 20th Sept., 1853, Mary, daughter of Thomas Knipe, of Hest Bank, near Lancaster, she died at Lancaster, 27th January, 1872; he married 2ndly in Feb., 1875, Mary Eleanor Nicholson; by his 1st wife he had 2 sons and a daughter:

(1) John Albright, of Ulverston, born at Lancaster, 22nd Sept., 1854; married at Whitehaven, 28th Dec. 1879, Sarah Jane Shippen of that place, and has a son and 3 daughters:

Thomas Albright
See Page 49.

Joseph Albright
See Page 50.

Edward C. Backhouse
See Page 15.

Henry Albright
See Page 50.

Owen Albright
See Page 51

(1) Joseph Albright, born 4th Oct., 1880.
(2) Mary Albright, born 23rd Oct., 1882.
(3) Catherine Albright, born 1st November, 1885.
(4) Margaret Albright, born 12th Sept., 1887.

(2) Joseph Pearson Albright, of Diss, born at Lancaster, 8th June, 1858; married in London, 23rd June, 1888, Ann Bowlt, daughter of William Gilhespie, and has 2 sons:

(1) Joseph Pearson Albright, born at Diss, 7th Nov., 1889.
(2) Thomas Knipe Albright, born at Diss, 14th Jan., 1891.

(3) Sarah Agnes Albright, born at Lancaster, 8th April, 1861.

(5) Mary Albright, born 1st Oct., 1817, died 8th March, 1829.

(6) William Whitlark Albright, of Sheffield, born 2nd Jan., 1819, died 2nd March, 1864; married at Sheffield 23rd Oct., 1851, Elizabeth, daughter of Jonathan Smith, of London, corn factor, and had at least 4 sons and 3 daughters:

(1) Sarah Albright, born 23rd Jan., 1853; married 1st Oct., 1887, to Charles A. Chambers, *s.p.*

(2) Peirson Albright, born 16th June, 1854.

(3) Anna Maria Albright, born 17th Jan., 1856, died 27th Aug., 1864.

(4) William Henry Albright, born 19th Aug., 1857; married 14th Sept., 1882, Alice Henley, of London.

(5) Edwin Albright, born 18th March, 1859, died 27th May, 1867.

(6) George Albright, born 15th March, 1861.

(7) Elizabeth Albright, born 10th August, 1863.

(7) Sarah Anne Albright, born 6th July, 1820, died 6th Nov., 1826.

(8) Charles Albright, born 14th Dec., 1821, died at Blythe, Notts, 14th Nov., 1841.

(9) Pearson Albright, born 29th Jan., 1823, died 16th April, 1843.

(10) James Albright, born 13th Feb., 1824, died 24th June, 1843.

(11) Edmund Albright, born 17th May, 1825, died 16th July following.

(12) Hannah Maria Albright, born 15th Aug., 1826; married to Joseph Tatum, of Salem Town, and died *s.p.* in America.

(13) Agnes Albright, born 30th Oct., 1827, died in America 30th Jan., 1854; married Games, and left a son and daughter.

(14) Edward Albright, in California, born 21st June, 1829.

(15) Owen Albright, of Florida, born 5th Oct., 1830, and has a son and 2 daughters.

(16) Frederick Albright, of Ohio, born 21st July, 1833.

(2 *c*) Mary Albright (daughter of John Albright and Agnes Pearson, see page 49), twin with Hannah, born 1784, vi. 15, died 1786, iii. 24.

(3 *c*) Hannah Albright, twin with Mary, died 1786, iv. 2.

(4 *c*) Mary Hannah Albright, born 1786, viii. 10, died 11th June, 1788.

(5 *c*) Sarah Albright, born 1788, iv. 21, died 10th Feb., 1790.

(6 *c*) Ann Albright, born 1789, vii. 11; died unmarried 11th Oct., 1867.

(7 *c*) Agnes Albright, born 1793, viii. 18, died unmarried 14th Nov. 1827, aged 34.

(5 *b*) Mary Pearson (daughter of Thomas and Hannah, see page 48), died 6th Dec., 1798, aged 48; married at Park End, in Preston Patrick, 1773, iv. 2, to Thomas Airey, of Burnley, mercer (son of John and Anne, of Kirby Kendal). He died at Burnley 31st Jan., 1798, having had 3 sons and 4 daughters:

(1) Joseph Airey, born 1st Oct., 1774, believed to have been carried off by the press-gang; living in 1804.

(2) Thomas Airey, of Macclesfield, brewer, born 7th June, 1776, married Ann Paxton, of Macclesfield, and died *s.p.* 4th Sept., 1847.

(3) Sarah Airey, born 6th June, 1778, died at Southport 7th Nov. 1863; married 1st to James Fishwick, of Burnley, and had a son, Richard, who died young; she re-married to Robert Blake Irving.

(4) Hannah Airey, born 4th Oct., 1780; married at Warrington 28th Feb., 1804, to James Kekwick, of Warrington, dyer, who died in Aug., 1835, having had 3 sons and 2 daughters:

(1) Daniel Kekwick, born 16th April, 1807, died 4th June, 1833.

(2) Mary Kekwick, born 15th March, 1809; died 15th Sept., 1890; married 19th May, 1836, to Rogers Broadhead, of Sheffield; he died 28th April, 1876, having had an only daughter:

Anna Maria Broadhead, born 3rd March, 1837; married 21st June, 1860, to George Henry Smith (son of Joseph and Mary Anne), of Sheffield, *s.p.*

(3) Thomas Kekwick, born 1st Jan., 1811, died 26th June, 1827.

(4) Elizabeth Kekwick, born 26th Dec., 1812, died 11th Jan., 1813.

(5) John Kekwick, of Cairnforth, near Rotherham, J.P., Yorks. (W.R.), patron of the advowson of Meare, Somerset, late commissioner of property and income tax, born 24th March, 1815; married 22nd Aug., 1848, Fanny, daughter of Thomas May, of Catcliffe, near Rotherham, and has had 2 daughters: [1876.

(1) Mary Isabella Kekwick, born 18th Sept., 1851, died 24th Jan.,

(2) Helen Beatrice Kekwick, born 14th June, 1853.

(5) Ann Airey, born 13th Jan., 1783, died at Brookside, Penketh, near

Warrington, 22nd March, 1874; married 3rd May, 1808, to Edward Bolton, of Warrington, ironmonger (son of Thomas Bolton and his wife Hannah Harrison), he was born 13th Nov., 1783, and died 13th April, 1840, having had 4 sons and 5 daughters, all born at Warrington (*d*):

(1 *d*) Mary Bolton, born 25th March, 1809, died unmarried 1st June, 1870.

(2 *d*) Ann Bolton, born 15th May, 1811, died in infancy.

(3 *d*) Thomas Bolton, born 18th March, 1813, died *s.p.* 8th Oct., 1874; married 6th April, 1837, Anne Platt Bradshaw, who died 29th July, 1866.

(4 *d*) James Bolton, of Warrington, born 27th Feb., 1815, died 20th March, 1859; married at Torquay 13th April, 1846, Henrietta, daughter of Thomas Crane, of Chester; she died 20th June, 1885, leaving 2 sons and 2 daughters, all born at Warrington:

(1) James Bolton, of Warrington, accountant, born 29th Jan., 1847; married at Leeds 16th Aug., 1877, Helen, daughter of Edward and Sarah (Frankland) Bolton, of Leeds, and has 5 sons and a daughter, all born at Warrington:

(1) Laurence Bolton, born 14th Aug., 1878.

(2) Frances Bolton, born 9th Jan., 1881.

(3) Eric Bolton, born 25th March, 1882.

(4) Geoffrey Bolton, born 15th Jan., 1884.

(5) Denys Bolton, born 3rd Feb., 1886, died 22nd Nov. [following.

(6) Austin Bolton, born 15th April, 1890.

(2) Henrietta Bolton, born 28th June, 1848.

(3) Elizabeth Ellen Bolton, born 5th Feb., 1854; married 26th May, 1875, to Hamlet Newhall Houghton.

(4) Charles Henry Bolton, born 29th July, 1856.

(5 *d*) Hannah Bolton, born 23rd Aug., 1816, died 25th Nov., 1882; married 4th April, 1839, to Benjamin Irlam Barlow, of Bishop Stortford, formerly of Hindley, co. Lanc.; he died 5th Dec., 1866, having had 4 sons and 5 daughters:

(1) Charles Edward Barlow, born 16th Oct., 1841; married 9th Aug., 1870, Alice Solton, daughter of Thomas Eskdale, of Great Sankey, co. Lanc., formerly of Whitby, and has had 4 sons and 2 daughters:

(1) Mary Alice Barlow, born 11th May, 1871.

(2) Arthur Eskdale Barlow, born 16th July, 1873.

(3) Frederic Irlam Barlow, born 17th July, 1875, died same year.

(4) Frank Edgar Barlow, born 26th May, 1877.

(5) Edith Annie Barlow, born 30th Nov., 1878.

(6) Charles Henry Barlow, born 13th June, 1882.

(2) Alice Jane Barlow, born 9th May, 1844.
(3) Arthur Bolton Barlow, born 28th Sept., 1845, died unmarried 14th Feb., 1879.
(4) Benjamin Irlam Barlow, born 23rd June, 1847; married 20th April, 1876, Cecilia Emily Baker, and has had 4 sons and 2 daughters:
(1) Emily Irlam Barlow, born 27th Jan., 1877.
(2) Alfred Irlam Barlow, born 12th Jan., 1878.
(3) Cyril Irlam Barlow, born 9th May, 1880.
(4) Harold Irlam Barlow, born 14th Dec., 1881.
(5) Mary Irlam Barlow, born 29th Nov., 1883, died 25th May, [1888.
(6) Stewart Irlam Barlow, born 29th May, 1889.
(5) Frances Louisa Barlow, born 28th July, 1848.
(6) Lucy Anna Barlow, born 12th Sept., 1849.
(7) Hannah Bolton Barlow, born 2nd Nov., 1851.
(8) Hubert John Barlow, born 16th Feb., 1853.
(9) Florence Elizabeth Barlow, born 7th April, 1855.

(6*d*) Lucy Bolton, born 29th Aug., 1818, died 18th Feb., 1890; married at Penketh, 24th June, 1846, to William Oddie, of Seacombe, near Liverpool; he died 9th Nov., 1864.

(7*d*) Jane Bolton, born 9th Nov., 1820; married at Penketh, 27th March, 1851, to George Worsdell, of Warrington, and has a son and 2 daughters, all born there:
(1) Edward Worsdell, B.A. London, born 21st March, 1852; married at Falmouth, 18th April, 1889, Rachel Tregelles, 3rd daughter of Nathaniel Fox, of Falmouth.
(2) Clara Jane Worsdell, born 30th March, 1854.
(3) Elizabeth Ann Worsdell, born 10th Aug., 1856.

(8*d*) Edward Bolton, born 19th Jan., 1823, died 26th Dec., 1889; married 13th May, 1846, Elizabeth Yates, of Eccleston, near St. Helens, and had 8 sons and 3 daughters:
(1) Edward Bolton, born 29th March, 1847, died 24th April, 1865.
(2) Mary Jane Bolton, born 5th Aug., 1848, died 18th Oct. 1876; married 1st June, 1870, to William Horace Wilson, Hon. Lieut.-Col. 43rd Regiment Light Infantry, formerly of 87th Foot, and had a son and daughter:
(1) Violet Eleanor Luxmore Wilson, born 1872.
(2) Horace Hayman Wilson, born 21st July, 1874.
(3) George Yates Bolton, Lieut.-Col. 1st volunteer battalion South Lancashire Regiment, born 22nd March, 1852; married

15th June, 1875, Margaret Ellen Hogarth, and had a son and daughter:

(1) Marian Ida Margaret Bolton, born 5th April, 1876.

(2) Richard Bolton, born 1879, died 1st Dec. same year.

(4) Charles Frederick Bolton, in Australia, born 4th Oct., 1853; married Louisa Oakden, and has 2 sons and a daughter:

(1) Edward Yates Bolton.

(2) Beatrice Bolton.

(3) Sydney Victor Bolton.

(5) William Henry Bolton, born 13th June, 1855.

(6) Alfred Bolton, born 22nd May, 1857.

(7) Frank Robinson Bolton, born 8th Nov., 1859.

(8) Edith Bolton, born 27th April, 1862, died 5th March, 1865.

(9) Annie Elizabeth Bolton, born 12th Aug., 1863.

(10) Walter Septimus Bolton, born 15th Jan., 1865.

(11) Ernest Edward Bolton, born 16th Oct., 1867, died 16th June, 1868.

(9 *d*) George Harrison Bolton, of Penketh, near Warrington, born 10th Oct. 1825; married 1st June, 1848, Wilhelmina, daughter of William Sproule, of Athlone, and has had 2 sons and 2 daughters:

(1) Ann Airey Bolton, born 17th June, 1849.

(2) Jane Sarah Bolton, born 21st Sept., 1850, married 21st Aug., 1877, to Josiah R. Wylde, of Runcorn, and has a son:

Claud Bolton Wylde, born 24th Jan., 1880.

(3) Edward Bolton, born 26th Dec., 1851, died 6 Oct., 1885; married 10th Sept., 1879, Charlotte Mary Hill, of Brooklyn, New York, and had 3 sons:

(1) Julius Duncan Bolton, born 5th Dec., 1880.

(2) Trevor Edward Bolton, born 5th July, 1883.

(3) son, born 4th Feb., 1885.

(4) George Harrison Bolton, born 28th Jan., 1853.

(6) John Airey, born 13th July, 1785, died unmarried at Southport, 3rd Jan., 1843.

(7) Mary Airey, born at Burnley 7th Sept., 1787, died unmarried at Southport, 20th Feb., 1860.

(6 *b*) Thomas Pearson, of Poolbank in Crosthwaite, parish of Heversham, Westmorland, yeoman (son of Thomas and Hannah, see p. 48), born 1753, xi. 12, died at Poolbank 3rd May, 1808, aged 55; he married Mary, daughter of Benjamin Hall, of Newton; she died 16th Jan., 1827, aged 87, having had at least 6 sons:

(1) Thomas Pearson, born 1776, iv. 29, died in London unmarried, twin with

(2) John Pearson, married twice, and died in America, leaving at least 4 sons by his 1st wife, viz.:

(1) John Pearson.

(2) Thomas Pearson.

(3) Isaac Pearson.

(4) Joseph Pearson, died at Pool Bank in 1874.

(3) Benjamin Pearson, of Kendal, born 1778, ix. 8, died 1846, leaving, by Gaskell, 4 daughters:

(1) Mary Ann Pearson.

(2) Betsy Pearson, married to John Warhurst, *s.p.*.

(3) Sarah Pearson, unmarried.

(4) Hannah Pearson, married to Capt. Rigby, and had 1 daughter: Sarah, who died leaving issue.

(4) Isaac Pearson, born 1782, vii. 7, married.

(5) George Pearson, born 1787, xi. 6, died 1st Jan., 1815, aged 27.

(6) Joseph Pearson, of Poolbank, yeoman, born 20th Aug., 1791, died 12th Feb., 1844; he married Mary, daughter of James Dodgson, of Swallowfield, Cartmel Fell; she died 24th July, 1833, aged 37, having had 2 sons and a daughter:

(1) Thomas Pearson, born 26th Sept., 1828, died *s.p.*, 4th May, 1872; married Margaret Jackson.

(2) Sarah Pearson, born 24th Jan., 1830, died 3rd Nov., 1830.

(3) George Pearson, of Poolbank in Crosthwaite, Kendal, born 4th April, 1832; married at Crosthwaite 4th April, 1860, Nancy, daughter of Thomas Lewis, of Rusmickle, in the township of Lyth, and has had 5 sons and a daughter:

(1) George Pearson, born 24th May, 1862, died March, 1863.

(2) Thomas Pearson, born 12th Feb., 1863.

(3) Joseph Pearson, born 23rd October, 1864.

(4) George Gibson Pearson Pearson, born 16th Jan., 1866, died 8th Dec., 1873.

(5) Mary Pearson, born 17th May, 1868.

(6) Benjamin Pearson, born 31st May, 1870.

BEAKBANE, FORMERLY OF LANCASTER.

SARAH CUMMING (2nd daughter of John Cumming, of Hilderstone, and Hannah Backhouse, his wife, see page 48), born 1689, x. 28, died 1764, i. 24, aged 74; married at Yealand 1711, viii. (or xi.) 10, to Thomas Beakbane, of Gunnerthwaite, parish of Melling, co. Lanc.; he died 1750, vii. 10, having had 4 sons and a daughter:

(1) Margaret Beakbane, born at Moss-side 1713, vi. 18, died 1729, vi. 2.

(2) Thomas Beakbane, of Arkholme, formerly of Gunnerthwaite, parish of Melling, co. Lanc., born 1717, viii. 29, died 14th July, 1788, aged 70.

(3) JOHN BEAKBANE, of whom presently.

(4) Robert Beakbane, died 1727, xii. 2.

(5) Robert Beakbane, born 1732, iii. 1.

JOHN BEAKBANE, of Lancaster, merchant, born there 1720, v. 3, and died there 1786, v. 14; married at Kendal 1750, v. 1, Mary, daughter of Jonathan Wilson of that place (and his wife Hannah, daughter of Roger Wakefield, of Kendal), and had a son and 3 daughters:

(1) Sarah Beakbane, married to Robert Waterhouse (see page 61).

(2) Hannah Beakbane, born at Lancaster, 1758, ii. 13 or 22, died 1778, iv. 15.

(3) Mary Beakbane, married to John Wakefield, of Kendal (see page 64).

(4) THOMAS BEAKBANE, of whom next.

THOMAS BEAKBANE, of Lancaster, born there 1760, died 16th March, 1839; married at Yealand 1796, ii. 3, Susannah, daughter of Thomas Frankland, of Lancaster; she died 26th Oct., 1843, aged 77, having had 4 sons and a daughter:

(1) John Beakbane, born at Lancaster 1796, xi. 5, died 2nd November, 1807.

(2) Henry Beakbane, born at Lancaster 1798, xii. 25, died there 15th May, 1869; married there 25th June, 1835, Rebecca, daughter of Robert Hall, of Skerton, co. Lancaster; she was born there, 25th Feb., 1796, and died at Chester 20th Dec., 1857, leaving an only son:

> HENRY HALL BEAKBANE, of Stourport, co. Worcester, born at Litherland 4th April, 1840; married at Lancaster 27th March, 1873, Ellen, eldest daughter of Isaac Bradshaw of that place; she was born 16th June, 1845, and has 2 sons and 5 daughters:

(1) Ellen Beakbane, born at Penketh 19th April, 1874.
(2) Sarah Elizabeth Beakbane, born at Penketh 9th July, 1875.
(3) Hannah Beakbane, born at Penketh 13th Dec., 1876.
(4) Henry Beakbane, born at Penketh 10th May, 1878.
(5) Edwin Beakbane, born at Warrington 25th Sept., 1879.
(6) Mary Edith Beakbane, born at Stourport 5th Jan., 1881.
(7) Florence Beakbane, born at Stourport 13th Sept., 1882.

(3) Thomas Beakbane, of Liverpool, tanner, born at Lancaster 31st Oct., 1804, and died at Liverpool 14th April, 1850; married there 2nd Dec., 1830, Eliza, daughter of William Holmes of Sutton Ashfield, Notts; she was born 29th Sept., 1803, and died 13th April, 1878, having had 7 sons and 3 daughters:

(1) Elizabeth Beakbane, born at Liverpool 23rd Sept., 1831, died 2nd July, 1836.

(2) William Fox Beakbane, migrated to Canada, born at Liverpool 8th Feb., 1833, died at Montreal 24th July, 1883; married at New York 10th June, 1861, Cecilia, daughter of Hynes, of New York, and had 7 sons and a daughter:

(1) Thomas William Beakbane, born 15th Dec., 1862.
(2) Eliza Beakbane, born 26th March, 1864, married in 1885.
(3) John Beakbane, of Jersey, born 20th Aug., 1865.
(4) James Beakbane, of Montreal, born 14th April, 1867.
(5) Walter Beakbane, of Portland, Oregon, born 18th June, 1869.
(6) Charles Edward Beakbane, born 6th June, 1871.
(7) Joseph Beakbane, born 7th July, 1872.
(8) Benjamin Beakbane, born 6th April, 1873.

(3) Thomas Frankland Beakbane, born at Liverpool 1st October, 1834, died 28th June, 1836.

(4) John Beakbane, born at Liverpool 5th June, 1836, died 3rd July following.

(5) Mary Beakbane, born at Everton 27th May, 1837, died in London 26th August, 1888; married at Liverpool, 22nd July, 1858, to Joseph Binyon Forster, son of Wilson Forster and his wife, Ann Binyon. He was born at Liverpool 23rd October, 1831, and died at Bowdon, Cheshire, 1st December, 1883, having had a son and 3 daughters:

(1) Eliza Mary Forster, born at Chorlton 29th May, 1859; married 6th November, 1884, to William Henry Cowie (son of David Cowie, of St. Vincent, W.I., and his wife, Charlotte Eliza Beresford); he was born 11th November, 1857, and has had 3 sons and 2 daughters:

(1) David Forster Cowie, born in Antigua 25th July, 1885.
(2) Eliza Wilhelmina Mary Cowie, born in Antigua 1st Aug., 1886, died in St. Christopher, W.I., 4th Jan., 1890.

(3) Joseph Beresford Cowie, born in London 2nd Nov., 1887; died in Antigua 28th Feb., 1888.

(4) Dorothea Cowie, born in St. Christopher 11th Feb., 1889.

(5) William Edward Christopher Cowie, born in St. Christopher 26th March, 1890.

(2) Joseph Wilson Forster, born at Chorlton 14th July, 1861.

(3) Josephine Binyon Forster, born at Altrincham 26th May, 1864.

(4) Annie Gulielma Forster, born at Altrincham 28th April, 1868.

(6) Thomas Beakbane, of Llay Place, Wrexham, born at Everton 15th June, 1839; married at Sale 2nd Sept., 1868, Lucy Anne, daughter of Nathaniel Card, of that place (and his wife, Hannah Binyon), and has had 2 sons and 2 daughters:

(1) Edith Beakbane, born at Sefton 18th Aug., 1869.

(2) Thomas Beakbane, born at Sefton 28th April, 1872, died 21st July following.

(3) Mary Anna Beakbane, born at Sefton 30th Oct., 1873.

(4) Thomas Card Beakbane, born at Gresford, co. Denbigh, 19th May, 1876.

(7) Frankland Beakbane, born at Everton 15th April, 1841, and died 15th Dec. following.

(8) Alfred Beakbane, born at Bootle 26th August, 1843, died 30th July, 1886; married 16th April, 1868, Eliza Fanny, daughter of Payne, of , and had 3 sons and a daughter:

(1) Alfred Bernard Beakbane, born at Seaforth 12th Sept., 1869.

(2) Charles Frankland Beakbane, born at Seaforth 11th Nov., 1873.

(3) Frances Mary Beakbane, born at Crosby 22nd March, 1878.

(4) Lionel St. George Beakbane, born at Crosby 17th Feb., 1882.

(9) Susan Ann Beakbane, born at Litherland 15th Sept., 1845; married at Liverpool 13th April, 1871, to Alfred (son of Thomas) Leicester; he was born at Liverpool 18th April, 1845, and has a son and 2 daughters, all born at Waterloo, near Liverpool:

(1) Eliza Mary Leicester, born 24th March, 1872.

(2) Alfred Charles Leicester, born 18th May, 1875.

(3) Jessie Leicester, born 27th November, 1880.

(10) Charles Beakbane, born at Litherland 1st Dec., 1847; unmarried.

(4) Elizabeth Beakbane, born at Liverpool, 6th January, 1808, died there 21st Jan., 1880.

(5) Edward Frankland Beakbane, born at Liverpool 13th Dec., 1813; married 30th Sept., 1845, Sarah Whittle, daughter of William Ockleston, of Wincham, Cheshire, and has had 2 sons and 3 daughters:

(1) Sarah Beakbane, born 9th October, 1848; married 30th Sept., 1868, to Robert Marquis, of Liverpool, and has 2 sons and 3 daughters:

(1) Marion Marquis, born at Liverpool 28th Feb., 1870.
(2) Robert Marquis, born at Liverpool 25th Aug., 1875.
(3) Lilian Marquis, born at Birkenhead 11th Dec., 1876.
(4) Edward Marquis, born at Birkenhead 26th Feb., 1879.
(5) Alice Marquis, born at Birkenhead 23rd Aug., 1880.

(2) Edward Beakbane, born 21st March, 1850, died 27th Jan., 1885.

(3) Lucy Beakbane, born 5th Dec., 1851; married 23rd May, 1878, to Alfred Woodall, of Liverpool, and has a son and 4 daughters, all born at Liverpool:

(1) Edward Arthur Woodall, born 20th June, 1879.
(2) Elsie Woodall, born 18th June, 1880.
(3) Gladys Woodall, born 29th Dec., 1882.
(4) Florence Woodall, born 27th Oct., 1885.
(5) Doris Woodall, born 25th Feb., 1892.

(4) Thomas William Beakbane, born 12th April, 1854; married at Bridgnorth, Salop, 5th Feb., 1880, Margaret, daughter of Samuel Harvey, of Walton on the Hill, co. Lanc., and has 2 daughters:

(1) Margaret Harvey Beakbane, born 25th July, 1887.
(2) Manzanita Harvey Beakbane, born 26th October, 1889.

(5) Florence Beakbane.

TAYLOR, OF LONDON.

SARAH BEAKBANE (eldest daughter of John Beakbane, of Lancaster, merchant, and his wife Mary Wilson, see page 57), born at Lancaster, 1751, iii. 2, died at Liverpool 8th April, 1820; married at Wray, near Lancaster, 1778, ix. 8, to Robert Waterhouse, of Colne (son of Joshua and Elizabeth Waterhouse); he was born at Liverpool, 1753, i. 20, and died before 1789, having had two sons and 4 daughters:

(1) Hannah Waterhouse, born 1779, vi. 12, died unmarried 26th Feb., 1855.

(2) Mary Waterhouse, born 1781, v. 6, died in London 6th Nov., 1850. She married 1st at Preston Patrick 9th August, 1802, to John Taylor, of Liverpool (son of Henry Taylor, of North Shields); he was born at the last-named place 1777, v. 4, and died at Liverpool 15th August, 1822. She re-married at Litherland, , 1825, to Benjamin Busby Binyon, who died at Sevenoaks, Kent, , 1865. By her 1st husband she had 5 sons and 5 daughters:

- (1) Ann Taylor, born 10th June, 1803, died 29th Jan., 1810.
- (2) Sarah Maria Taylor, born 23rd Jan., 1805, died 17th Sept., 1823.
- (3) Eliza Taylor, born 7th Oct., 1806, and died unmarried 8th Jan., 1870.
- (4) Henry Taylor, born 17th Dec., 1807, died 7th Jan., 1874; married in London 3rd December, 1844, Eliza Snoad, of Brookland, Kent. She was born 5th August, 1824, and died in April, 1885, having had 3 sons and 4 daughters, all born in London:
  - (1) Henrietta Eliza Taylor, born at Peckham 13th Sept., 1846, died 13th Oct., 1849.
  - (2) Anne Maria Taylor, born at Peckham 17th April, 1848; married July, 1867 to Capt. Henry Augustus Chichele Plowden, Bengal Staff Corps, barrister-at-law, Middle Temple, 1876, who died 10th March, 1877. She re-married 25th Nov., 1880, to John Robson, of London. By her 1st husband she had 2 sons and 2 daughters:
    - (1) Millicent Chichele Plowden, born 11th Jan., 1870, died in India, Aug., 1872.
    - (2) Roger Augustus Chichele Plowden, born at Moradabad, Calcutta, 20th Oct., 1871.
    - (3) Henry Launcelot Chichele Plowden, born 3rd Oct., 1873, died in India, 15th June, 1874.
    - (4) Henrietta Annie Chichele Plowden, born in London, 2nd Sept., 1875.

(3) John Henry Taylor, born at Peckham 7th June, 1849; married 28th April, 1875, Lilla, daughter of George Hearn, of Highbury, and has a son and 2 daughters, all born in London:

(1) Violet Taylor, born 14th March, 1876.

(2) Eva Alexina Snoad Taylor, born 31st Oct., 1877.

(3) Claude Waterhouse Hearn Taylor, born 19th Oct., 1880.

(4) Eliza Emily Taylor, born at Maida Vale 26th Nov., 1850; married 18th July, 1872, to Charles Dennis Hoblyn, of London, stockbroker, and has 3 sons and 5 daughters:

(1) Beatrice Mary Dennis Hoblyn, born 9th Dec., 1873.

(2) Reginald Armstrong Hoblyn, born 6th Sept., 1875.

(3) Lizzie Evelyn Hoblyn, born 27th Feb., 1877.

(4) Gertrude Florence Hoblyn, born 5th Feb., 1880.

(5) Dora Dennis Hoblyn, born 26th Dec., 1881.

(6) Charles William Thornton Hoblyn, born 29th March, 1885.

(7) Phyllis Sherwood Hoblyn, born 11th Dec., 1886.

(8) Harry Beverley Hoblyn, born 18th Sept., 1888.

(5) Mary Jane Taylor, born 30th Aug., 1852, died 3rd Dec., 1870.

(6) William Charles Taylor, of Twickenham, born at Maida Vale, 29th March, 1854; married , 1879, Eleanor, daughter of Alfred Froom, and has a son and 2 daughters:

(1) Millicent Vernon Taylor, born

(2) Muriel Valèrie Maud Taylor, born

(3) Eric William Waterhouse Taylor, born

(7) Alfred Waterhouse Somerset Taylor, born at Maida Vale 8th March, 1862.

(5) Mary Taylor, born 17th May, 1809, died 4th Nov., 1824.

(6) William Taylor, born 17th Nov., 1810, died 23rd July, 1842; married 1841, Caroline B. Moffatt, and had a son:

Henry George Moffatt Taylor, born 26th Sept., 1841.

(7) John Taylor, born 28th Aug., 1812, died *s.p.* 2nd Oct., 1878; married 5th Jan., 1856, Susan Haselden.

(8) Anne Taylor, born 8th March, 1815; married at Camberwell 11th April, 1846, to Joseph Churchill, of London (son of Joseph Churchill, of London); he was born 29th Jan., 1812, and died 3rd July, 1881, leaving a son and daughter:

(1) Florence Churchill Churchill, born in London 5th Feb., 1847; married 1st Feb., 1877, to John Hampton Hale, of London, and has 2 sons and a daughter:

(1) Nora Florence Hale, born in London 2nd April, 1878.

(2) Horace John Hale, born in London 21st Jan., 1880.

(3) Walter Churchill Hale, born in London 12th Aug., 1881.

(2) John Churchill, born in London 25th Jan., 1852; married at Sydenham 12th June, 1883, Florence Ida Josephine, daughter of Andreas Christian Friedrich Gerich, of London, and has had 2 daughters:

(1) Florence Elfrida Grace Churchill, born 5th April, 1884, died 30th Nov., 1889.

(2) Irene Josephine Churchill, born 18th Dec., 1887.

(9) Edward Taylor, born 31st Dec., 1816, died young.

(10) Robert Taylor, born 31st Dec., 1816, died young.

(3) Charles Waterhouse, born 1782, xii. 24, died 2nd June, 1818.

(4) Elizabeth Waterhouse, born 1785, v. 8, died at Peckham, Surrey, 5th Jan., 1849; married at Hardshaw, co. Lanc., 12th Feb., 1827, as 2nd wife to William Johnson (son of Daniel Johnson, of Ulverston); he was born 1771, viii. 9, and died in Manchester about 13th Feb., 1845.

(5) Henry Waterhouse, born 1787, ii. 3, died unmarried.

(6) Rachel Waterhouse, born 28th Jan., 1789, died in Jersey about March, 1853, and buried there; married to Richard Treffry, who died in Manchester about 1840, having had a son and 2 daughters:

(1) Waterhouse Treffry.

(2) Sarah Treffry.

(3) Hannah Treffry, married in 1853 to John Thomas Coudray, of Guernsey, and had 2 children.

WAKEFIELD, OF KENDAL.

MARY BEAKBANE, 3rd and youngest daughter of John Beakbane, of Lancaster, merchant, by his wife Mary Wilson (see page 57); died 10th Feb., 1824. She married at or near Sawley, Yorks, 16th May, 1787, to John Wakefield, of Kendal, banker (son of John Wakefield and his wife Margaret Hodgson, of Carlisle); he was born at Kendal 1761, iii. 13, and died there 30th Oct., 1829, having had 4 sons and 6 daughters:

(1) Isabella Wakefield, born 29th June, 1788, died 6th June, 1801.

(2) Margaret Wakefield, born 27th Oct., 1789, died unmarried June, 1862.

(3) John Wakefield, born 18th May, and died 7th July, 1791.

(4) Mary Wakefield, born 6th Dec., 1792, died unmarried , 1868.

(5) JOHN WAKEFIELD, of whom see page 70.

(6) Ann Wakefield, born 10th April, 1797, died 20th Sept., 1876; married at Preston Patrick 11th Jan., 1821, to John Cropper, of Dingle Bank, Liverpool (son of James Cropper and his wife Mary Brinsdon); he was born at Liverpool 8th June, 1797, and died there 8th Nov., 1874, having had 3 sons and 6 daughters, all born at Liverpool:

- (1) Mary Cropper, born 2nd Nov., 1821, died 30th Dec., 1885; married 25th Sept., 1851, to Very Rev. John Saul Howson, B.A. from Trin. Coll., Camb. (wrangler), 1837; M.A., 1841; D.D., 1861; Hulsean lecturer, 1862; Dean of Chester, 1867-85; Chaplain to the Bishop of Ely, 1865; Principal of Liverpool College, 1849-67; joint author of the "Life and Epistles of St. Paul." He died 15th Dec., 1885, having had 3 sons and 2 daughters:
  - (1) Mary Georgina Howson, born 1st Jan., 1853.
  - (2) George John Howson, M.A. from Trin. Coll., Camb., 1880; Vicar of Christ Church, Crewe, 1888; born 1st May, 1854; married 8th Jan., 1880, Ethel, daughter of Ven. Archdeacon Dealtry, Vicar of Maidstone, and has had 4 sons and a daughter:
    - (1) John Dealtry Howson, born 30th Dec., 1880, died in infancy.
    - (2) Roger Saul Howson, born 8th May, 1882.
    - (3) Geoffrey Howson, born 14th August, 1883.
    - (4) George Arthur Howson, born 7th Sept., 1886.
    - (5) Joan Howson, born 9th May, 1885.
  - (3) Edmund Whytehead Howson, M.A. from King's Coll., Camb., 1881, fellow 1882; Master at Harrow; born 18th July, 1855; married 14th Sept., 1886, Agnes, daughter of Rev. Henry Montagu Butler, D.D., Master of Trin. Coll., Camb., and has a son and daughter:
    - (1) Hugh Edmund Elliot Howson, born 20th Feb., 1889.
    - (2) Audrey Howson, born 6th July, 1891.

Dean Howson
Died, 1885.

Mrs Howson
1821-1885.

George J Howson

Edmund W Howson

(4) James Francis Howson, M.A. from Trin. Coll., Camb., 1882; Vicar of Christ Church, Chester, 1889; born 20th Sept., 1856.

(5) Anne Margaret Howson, born 20th Aug., 1858.

(2) James Cropper, of Eller Green, Kendal, M.P. 1880-85; J.P., D.L., Westmorland; High Sheriff, 1875; born 22nd Feb., 1823; married at Heversham 25th Nov., 1845, to his cousin Fanny Alison, 2nd daughter of John Wakefield, of Sedgwick House (see page 71); she died 3rd Feb., 1868, leaving a son and 2 daughters:

(1) Frances Anne Cropper, married 29th Dec., 1870, to Rev. John William Edward Conybeare, M.A. from Trin. Coll., Camb., Vicar of Barrington, co. Cambridge, since 1871, and has 3 sons and 2 daughters:

(1) William James Conybeare, born 19th Dec., 1871.

(2) Charles Bruce Conybeare, born 16th Feb., 1873.

(3) Alfred Edward Conybeare, born 25th August, 1875.

(4) Alison Mary Conybeare, born 26th March, 1879.

(5) Dorothea Frances Conybeare, born 18th Dec., 1880.

(2) Mary Wakefield Cropper.

(3) Charles James Cropper, of Tolson Hall, Westmorland, D.L.; B.A. from Trin. Coll., Camb.; born 6th July, 1852; married 3rd August, 1876, Hon. Edith Emily Holland, eldest daughter of Henry Thurstan, Lord Knutsford, G.C.M.G., Colonial Secretary 1886-92, and has a son and 4 daughters:

(1) James Winstanley Cropper, born 4th August, 1879.

(2) Eleanor Margaret Cropper.

(3) Mary Frances Cropper.

(4) Margaret Beatrice Cropper, born 29th Aug., 1886.

(5) Sybil Edith Cropper.

(3) Sarah Wakefield Cropper, born 11th July, 1824, died 21st June, 1890; married 6th Sept., 1849, to Rev. Arthur Willink, M.A. from St. John's Coll., Camb., 1849; Vicar of St. Paul's, Tranmere, Cheshire, 1857, until his death at Madeira, 21st Nov., 1862, having had 6 sons and 2 daughters:

(1) Arthur Willink, M.A. from Emanuel Coll., Camb., 1876, Curate of St. John the Evangelist, Bromley, 1889; born 1st July, 1850; married 2nd July, 1878, Margaret, daughter of Rev. Richard Henry Dickson, Rector of Eastchurch, Kent, and has had 3 sons and 2 daughters:

(1) Margaret Dorothea Rose Willink, born at Cambridge 29th Sept., 1879.

(2) Arthur Charles Eric Willink, born at Lindale, in Cartmel, 28th Jan., 1881.

(3) Hilda Mary Willink, born at Lindale 19th May, 1883.

(4) Herman James Lindall Willink, born at Lindale 14th Sept., 1884.

(5) Roger Jan Willink, born at Lindale 4th October, 1886, died 4th Dec., 1887.

(2) Clara Cecilia Willink, born 23rd March, 1852; married 28th July, 1881, to Rev. Norman Frederick McNeile, M.A., Vicar of Brafferton, Yorks, 1876 (son of late Hugh McNeile, D.D., Dean of Ripon).

(3) James Cropper Willink, born 7th June, 1853, died June, 1876.

(4) Charles Daniel Willink, born 3rd Nov., 1854, died 19th July, 1860.

(5) William Edward Willink, of Dingle Bank, Liverpool, M.A. from King's Coll., Camb., 1884; born 17th March, 1856; married 16th February, 1893, Florence Macan, youngest daughter of Col. H. Brabazon Urmston, Bengal S.C., and of Ardenlee, Maidstone.

(6) John Wakefield Willink, M.A. from Pembroke Coll., Camb., 1884, Vicar of St. Helens, Lancashire, 1891, and of St. John's, Sunderland, 1885-90; born 24th Oct., 1858; married 27th July, 1887, Ruth Agnes, daughter of J. D. Sim, Esq., C.S.I., late President of Council at Madras, and has a son and daughter:

(1) Arthur James Wakefield Willink, born 17th May, 1890.

(2) Mary Cecilia Wakefield Willink, born 2nd July, 1893.

(7) Alfred Henry Willink, born 24th May, 1860; married 16th April, 1885, Beatrice Amy, daughter of Major Luard-Selby, of the Mote, Ightham, Kent.

(8) Amelia Trevor Roper Willink, born 8th Sept., 1861, died Aug. 1862.

(4) Anne Cropper, born 20th Sept., 1825; married at Liverpool 7th May, 1850, to Thomas, son of Duncan Matheson, and nephew of late Sir James Matheson, Bart., of the island of Lews, N.B.

(5) John Wakefield Cropper, of Dingle Bank, Liverpool, born 24th March, 1830; died 3rd June, 1892; married at Rydal, Westmorland, 23rd August, 1853, Susanna Elizabeth Lydia, 3rd daughter of late Dr. Arnold, of Rugby.

(6) Isabella Cropper, born 13th May, 1831, and died 1st Aug. following.

(7) Edward William Cropper, of Fearnhead, Great Crosby, Cheshire, born 7th July, 1833; married at Ratcliffe-on-Trent 30th May, 1861, Frances, 2nd daughter of Ichabod Charles Wright, of Mapperley, Notts (by his wife, Hon. Theodosia, daughter of Thomas, 1st Lord Denman), and has had 5 sons and 5 daughters:

(1) James Cropper, B.A. from Trin. Coll., Camb., 1885, Vicar of St. Thomas, West Ham, Stratford, E., 1890; born at Thornton Fields, Guisboro', Yorks, 2nd May, 1862; married at Tunbridge Wells, 8th March, 1888, Ethel Frances, daughter of George Percival Smith, of Tunbridge Wells.

(2) Frances Mildred Theodosia Cropper, born at Thornton Fields, 23rd July 1863; married at Great Crosby, 27th January, 1889, to C. Theodore Green, M.R.C.S. and M.R.C.P.

(3) John Cropper, M.A. from Trin. Coll., Camb., 1891; B. Med., 1892; born at Thornton Fields 17th Sept., 1864.

Wakefield, of Birklands, Kendal.

John Backhouse, of Moss-side near Yealand Redman, co. Lanc., yeoman, died in 1690. See page 13. = Sarah, daughter of William Jackson, of Yealand Redmayne, by his wife Mabel, heiress of her brother John Carr, of Ridgend, in Mansergh, born about 1626, died 1706.

A

Hannah Backhouse, born 1658, died 1729. = John Cumming, of Hilderstone, mar. 1682, died in 1697.

Thomas Backhouse, of Yealand Redman, born 1661, died 1729. = Alice, daughter of Richard Becke, of Wythmore in Westmorland, mar. 1696, died 1700. See page 13.

Sarah Backhouse, born 1664, mar. 1688, died 1697, 1st wife. = George Robinson, of Yealand Conyers, died 1719. See page 14.

James Backhouse, of Yealand Conyers, born 1668, died in Lancaster Castle, 1697 (1st husband). = Janet, daughter of John Godsalve, of Yealand Conyers, mar. 1691. See page 14. = John Robinson, of Yealand, mar. 1701, 2nd husband.

Ann Cumming, born 1686, mar. (1st wife) 1717, died 1722. = John Lancaster, of Wray. See page 48.

Edward Cumming, of Hilderstone, born 1688, mar. 1720, died 1771. = Ann Sill, born about 1697, died 1761.

Sarah Cumming, born 1689, mar. 1711, died 1764. = Thomas Beakbane, of Gunnerthwaite, parish of Melling, co. Lanc., died 1750.

Hannah Cumming, mar. 1740, died 1771. = Thomas Pearson, of Powbank, or Poolbank, Westmorland, yeoman, died 1771. See page 48.

John Beakbane, of Lancaster, merchant, born 1720, died 1786. = Mary, daughter of Jonathan Wilson, of Kendal, mar. 1750.

Sarah Beakbane, born at Lancaster, 1751, mar. 1778, died 1820. = Robert Waterhouse, of Colne, born at Liverpool, 1753, died before 1789. See page 61.

Mary Beakbane, mar. 1787, died 1824. = John Wakefield, of Kendal, banker, born 1761, died 1829.

Thomas Beakbane, of Lancaster, born there 1760, mar. 1796, died 1839. = Susannah, daughter of Thomas Frankland, of Lancaster. See page 57.

John Wakefield, of Sedgwick House, Kendal, banker, High Sheriff of Westmorland, 1854, born 1794, died 1866. = Fanny, daughter of Dr. McArthur, of Glasgow, mar. 1823. See page 71.

Ann Wakefield, born 1797, mar. 1821, died 1876. = John Cropper, of Dingle Bank, Liverpool, born 1797, died 1874. See page 64.

Edward William Wakefield, of Kendal, banker, born 1792, died 1858. = Susanna, eldest daughter of William Birkbeck, of Settle, Yorks, banker, mar. 1822.

William Wakefield, of Birklands, Kendal, born 1825, mar. 1861, died 1893. = Marianne, daughter of E. M. Wavell, of Field House, Halifax.

Thomas Birkbeck Wakefield, of the Hall, Moate, co. Westmeath, born 1828. = Sophia Espinette, of Neufchatel, mar. 1849.

John Edward Wakefield, born 1830, mar. 1854, died 1858. = Rachel Crewdson, daughter of Henry Fox, of Tonedale, Wellington, Somerset; she died 1887.

George Henry Wakefield, of Wavertree, Liverpool, born 1835, mar. 1858. = Susan, daughter of Stafford S. Baxter, of Mancetter Manor, Atherstone.

Edward William Wakefield, born 1862, mar. 1886, Mary E., daughter of J. R. Wilkinson, of Skipton, Yorks.

Marian Alice Wakefield, born 1887.

Roger Wakefield, born 1865.
William B. Wakefield, born 1867.
Marianne I. Wakefield, born 1869.
Rachel M. Wakefield, born 1873.
Arthur William Wakefield.
Frances M. Wakefield, born 1879.

Eva Margaret Wakefield, mar. 1877, to John C. Rainey, have 8 children. See p. 69.
Ada Sophia Wakefield, mar. 1879, to Herbert Knott, of Stalybridge, have 3 children. See page 70.

Kathleen Jemima Wakefield, mar. 1878, to Edward Ffrench, M.D., and has issue. See page 70.
Edward Wakefield, born 1862, mar. 1878, Frances Conolly. =

Roger, born 1892. See page 70.

Rachel Mary Wakefield, mar. 1878, to Christopher Elliott, M.D. = See page 70.

John Edward William Wakefield, of Taunton, banker, born 1858, mar. 1882, Nora, 2nd daughter, of late Richard Drake. See page 70.

Mary Constance Wakefield, mar. 1882, to Capt. George M Saunders. See page 70.

(4) Charles Henry Edward Cropper, born 25th January, 1866.

(5) Edward Neville Cropper, born 14th May, 1869, died young.

(6) Frederick William Cropper, born at West Highfield 1st Feb., 1871.

(7) Mary Isabella Cropper, born 7th Jan., 1875, died young.

(8) Ann Wakefield Cropper, born at Bramcote, Great Crosby, 26th March, 1876.

(9) Emily Mabel Cropper, born at Bramcote 31st Dec., 1877.

(10) Evelyn Wright Cropper, born at Fearnhead, Great Crosby, 17th Nov., 1880.

(8) Isabella Eliza Cropper, born 7th May, 1835; married at Liverpool 4th Oct., 1854, to James Rigg Brougham, a registrar of the High Court of Justice (Bankruptcy division), and nephew of Henry Peter, 1st Lord Brougham, and has 2 sons and 5 daughters:

(1) Margaret Lyndesay Brougham, married 21st March, 1877, to Samuel Logan, eldest son of Carruthers Charles Johnston, of Liverpool, and has 4 sons and 3 daughters:

(1) Alfred Hubert Johnston, born 10th Feb., 1878.

(2) Carruthers Brougham Johnston, born 3rd June, 1879.

(3) Gladys Beryl Johnston, born 28th Jan., 1881.

(4) Leslie Darrell Johnston, born 29th May, 1883.

(5) Alexander Vyvyan Johnston, born 3rd Dec., 1884.

(6) Kathleen Stella Johnston, born 9th Nov., 1886.

(7) Olive Marjory Johnston, born 28th Aug., 1890.

(2) John Cropper Brougham, born 2nd Feb., 1857; married 26th Jan., 1882, Ursula Harriet Mary, younger daughter of late Sir Henry Orlando Chamberlain, Bart., and has at least a son and 2 daughters:

(1) James Henry Chamberlain Brougham, born 9th Dec., 1882.

(2) Constance Murielle Brougham, born 17th Sept., 1884.

(3) Gwendoline Islay Brougham, born at Elmwood, Hackbridge, Surrey, 29th August, 1892.

(3) Annie Wakefield Brougham, married 27th April, 1887, to Jacob, 2nd son of William Henry Wakefield, of Sedgwick House, Kendal (see page 71), and has a son:

William Henry Wakefield, born 6th Jan., 1891.

(4) Harold de Vaux Brougham, barrister-at-law, Lincoln's Inn, 1881, born 17th Aug., 1858.

(5) Kate Brougham, married 8th Jan., 1890, to John Wakefield Weston, Esq. (see page 71) and has a daughter:

Mary Elizabeth Weston, born 8th April, 1892.

(6) Eleanor Brougham.

(7) Mary Brougham.

William Wakefield
1825-1893.

Thomas B. Wakefield.

Edward William Wakefield.
1799-1838.

John E. Wakefield
See Page 70.

George H. Wakefield
See Page 70.

(9) Margaret Cropper, born 14th July, 1836; married 12th July, 1866, to Rev. William Jones, M.A. from Trinity College, Cambridge, 1860, Perpetual Curate of Burneside, Kendal, since 1869, Vicar of Burton-on-Trent, 1860-69, and has had 3 sons and 3 daughters:

(1) Agnes Harriet Jones, born 30th Nov., 1868, died 7th Jan., 1887.
(2) Herbert Gresford Jones, born 7th April, 1870.
(3) Vincent Strickland Jones, born 15th Feb., 1874.
(4) Alice Margaret Jones, born 1st April, 1875.
(5) Edith Winifred Jones, born 17th Dec., 1878.
(6) Clement Wakefield Jones, born 26th June, 1880.

(7) Edward William Wakefield, of Kendal, banker, born 7th Oct., 1799, died 6th Feb., 1858; married 3rd July, 1822, Susanna, eldest daughter of William Birkbeck, of Settle, Yorkshire, banker, and had 4 sons:

(1) William Wakefield, of Birklands, Kendal, banker, J.P., D.L., Westmorland, Chairman of Quarter Sessions, born 30th April, 1825, died 19th April, 1893; married 16th Oct., 1861, Marianne, daughter of E. M. Wavell, of Field House, Halifax, and has had 5 sons and 3 daughters:

(1) Edward William Wakefield, born 8th Sept., 1862; married 8th Sept., 1886, Mary, 2nd daughter of J. R. Wilkinson, of Skipton, Yorks, and has a daughter:
Marian Alice Wakefield, born 6th July, 1887.
(2) George Henry Wakefield, born 10th Aug., 1864, died 29th April, 1868.
(3) Roger William Wakefield, born 1st Nov., 1865.
(4) William Birkbeck Wakefield, born 9th Aug., 1867.
(5) Marianne Isabel Wakefield, born 31st Aug., 1869.
(6) Rachel Mary Wakefield, born 1st Feb., 1873.
(7) Arthur William Wakefield, born 13th April, 1876.
(8) Frances Margaret Wakefield, born 14th May, 1879.

(2) Thomas Birkbeck Wakefield, of the Hall, Moate, co. Westmeath, born 3rd Sept., 1828; married 15th May, 1849, Sophia Espinette, of Neufchatel, and has had a son and 4 daughters:

(1) Edith Susan Wakefield, born 20th March, 1850, died Dec., 1873.
(2) Eva Margaret Wakefield, married 20th March, 1877, to John Crofton Rainey, and has had 5 sons and 3 daughters:

(1) Arthur Pigou Rainey, born at Wellington, Somerset, 21st March, 1878.
(2) Annie Margaret Rainey, born at Wellington 18th Jan., 1879, died 18th Jan., 1879.
(3) John Wakefield Rainey, born at Totnes 31st Dec., 1881.
(4) James Henry Rainey, born at Totnes 18th June, 1883, died 18th June, 1883.
(5) Kathleen Emma Rainey, born at Totnes 17th June, 1884, died 10th May, 1889.

(6) Edward Holmes Rainey, born at Paignton, Devonshire, 5th April, 1886.

(7) Herbert ffrench Rainey, born at Paignton 19th Dec., 1888.

(8) Eva Marjorie Rainey, born at Paignton 21st Sept., 1890.

(3) Ada Sophia Wakefield, married at Dublin, 19th Sept., 1879, to Herbert Knott, of Stalybridge, and has 4 sons, born at Stalybridge:

(1) John Espinet Knott, born Jan., 1884.

(2) Cyril Wakefield Knott, born April, 1886.

(3) Roger Birkbeck Knott, born April, 1888.

(4) Frederick William Knott, born Feb., 1892.

(4) Kathleen Jemima Wakefield, married at Kilkenny West, 11th April, 1878, to Edward ffrench, M.D., of Glasson, co. Westmeath, and has 2 daughters:

(1) Eily Kathleen ffrench, born at Glasson 19th April, 1879.

(2) Ethel J. A. ffrench, born at Glasson 2nd May, 1882.

(5) Edward Wakefield, born at Kendal, 2nd June, 1862; married at Dublin, 14th May, 1891, Frances Alice, daughter of Owen Thomas Conolly, of Dublin, and has a son:

Roger Owen Birkbeck Wakefield, born at Farnagh, Moate, 20th July, 1892.

(3) John Edward Wakefield, born at Kendal 8th Aug., 1830, died at Malvern 30th July, 1858; married at Wellington 13th Sept., 1854, Rachel Crewdson, daughter of Henry Fox, of Tonedale, Wellington, Somerset. She died at Clifton 20th Sept., 1887, having had a son and daughter:

(1) Rachel Mary Wakefield, born at Ventnor 4th Oct., 1856; married 25th April, 1878, to Christopher Elliott, of Clifton, co. Glouc., D. Med., and has 3 sons and 2 daughters:

(1) Rachel Winifred Elliott, born 23rd May, 1880.

(2) Mary Dorothy Elliott, born 14th Sept., 1881.

(3) John Wakefield Elliott, born 14th May, 1884.

(4) Henry Christopher Elliott, born 23rd May, 1887.

(5) Edward Crewdson Elliott, born 5th Nov., 1888.

(2) John Edward William Wakefield, of Taunton, Solicitor, born at Ventnor, 31st March, 1858; married 9th Aug., 1882, Nora, 2nd daughter of late Richard Drake, Esq., and has a son and 2 daughters:

(1) Norah Muriel Wakefield, born 25th May, 1883.

(2) Cicely Corner Wakefield, born 5th Nov., 1884.

(3) John Hylbert Wakefield, born 9th Oct., 1886.

(4) George Henry Wakefield, of Wavertree, Liverpool, born 29th April, 1835; married 31st Aug., 1858, Susan, daughter of Stafford Stratton Baxter, of Mancetter Manor, Atherstone, and has had 4 daughters:

(1) Mary Constance Wakefield, married 19th Jan., 1882, to George Morley Saunders, Capt. Durham Light Infantry, Adjutant 3rd and 4th battalions Duke of Wellington's West Riding Regiment, 1885, and has a son:

Alan Morley Saunders, born April, 1885.

(2) Maude Wakefield, died 23rd Nov., 1888.

(3) Ethel Wakefield, died 24th March, 1889.

(4) Trixie Wakefield, died 4th Nov., 1888.

(8) William Henry Wakefield, born 25th Feb., 1804, died 3rd Aug., 1827.

(9) Isabella Wakefield, died *s.p.* 27th Sept., 1830, having married 18th Sept., 1821, as 1st wife to Edward Cropper, of Swaylands, Kent, who died 23rd May, 1877.

(10) Sarah Wakefield, born 29th Sept., 1807, died 22nd Aug., 1822.

JOHN WAKEFIELD, of Sedgwick House, Kendal, banker, High Sheriff, Westmorland, 1854 (eldest surviving son of John Wakefield and Mary Beakbane, see page 64), born 1st June, 1794, died 8th April, 1866; married at Glasgow 30th June, 1823, Fanny, daughter of Dr. McArthur, of Glasgow, she died 1832, aged 31, having had 2 sons and 4 daughters:

(1) Mary Wakefield, born 30th April, 1824, died 30th Nov., 1855; married 19th Sept., 1848, to Rev. George Frederick Weston, M.A. from Christ College, Camb., Vicar of Crosby Ravensworth, 1848, until he died, 14th Nov., 1887, having had a son and 2 daughters:

(1) Frances Elizabeth Weston, born 24th July, 1849, died 11th Feb., 1894; married at Crosby Ravensworth 30th Aug., 1870, to Rev. George Herbert Lightfoot, M.A. from Magdalen College, Oxon, Vicar of Pickering, Yorks, since 1881 (3rd son of Rev. John Prideaux Lightfoot, D.D., Rector of Exeter College, Oxon, 1854-87, and Vice-Chancellor 1862-66), and had an only son:

John Prideaux Lightfoot, born 4th Aug., 1871.

(2) Emily Margaret Weston, married 1st July, 1880, to Constantine William Benson, Esq., of Milnthorpe, and has a son and 2 daughters:

(1) Robert Benson, born at Crosby Ravensworth 20th May, 1881.

(2) Mary Wakefield Benson, born at Sibley, Osceola co., Iowa, U.S.A., 26th Dec., 1884.

(3) Eleanor Osceola Benson, born in Kensington 15th Feb., 1888.

(3) John Wakefield Weston, born 13th June, 1852; married 8th Jan., 1890, Kate, 3rd daughter of James Rigg Brougham, Esq. (see page 68), and has a daughter:

Mary Elizabeth Weston, born 8th April, 1892.

(2) Jacob Wakefield, born 3rd Sept., 1826, died young.

(3) Fanny Alison Wakefield, died 3rd Feb., 1868, having married at Heversham 25th Nov., 1860, to her cousin, James Cropper, Esq., of Eller Green, Kendal, and had a son and 2 daughters (see page 65).

Wakefield, of Sedgwick House, Kendal.

John Backhouse, of Moss-side near Yealand Redman, co. Lanc., yeoman, died in 1690. See page 13. = Sarah, daughter of William Jackson, of Yealand Redmayne, by his wife Mabel, heiress of her brother John Carr, of Ridgend, in Mansergh, born about 1626, died 1706.

A
Hannah Backhouse, born 1658, died 1729. = John Cumming, of Hilderstone, mar. 1682, died in 1697.

Thomas Backhouse, of Yealand Redman, born 1661, died 1729. = Alice, daughter of Richard Becke, of Wythmore in Westmorland, mar. 1696, died 1700.
See page 13.

Sarah Backhouse, born 1664, mar. 1688, died 1697, 1st wife. = George Robinson, of Yealand Conyers, died 1719.
See page 14.

James Backhouse, of Yealand Conyers, born 1668, died in Lancaster Castle, 1697 (1st husband). = Janet, daughter of John Godsalve, of Yealand Conyers, mar. 1691. = John Robinson, of Yealand, mar. 1701, 2nd husband.
See page 14.

Ann Cumming, born 1686, mar. 1717 (1st wife), died 1722. = John Lancaster, of Wray.
See page 48.

Edward Cumming, of Hilderstone, born 1688, mar. 1720, died 1771. = Ann Sill, born about 1697, died 1761.

Sarah Cumming, born 1689, mar. 1711, died 1764. = Thomas Beakbane, of Gunnerthwaite, parish of Melling, co. Lanc., died 1750.

Hannah Cumming, mar. 1740, died 1771. = Thomas Pearson, of Powbank, or Poolbank, Westmorland, yeoman, died 1771.
See page 48.

John Beakbane, of Lancaster, merchant, born 1720, died 1786. = Mary, daughter of Jonathan Wilson, of Kendal, mar. 1750.

Sarah Beakbane, born at Lancaster, 1751, mar. 1778, died 1820. = Robert Waterhouse, of Colne, born at Liverpool, 1753, died before 1789.
See page 61.

Mary Beakbane, mar. 1787, died 1824. = John Wakefield, of Kendal, banker, born 1761, died 1829.

Thomas Beakbane, of Lancaster, born there 1760, mar. 1796, died 1839. = Susannah, daughter of Thomas Frankland, of Lancaster.
See page 57.

John Wakefield, of Sedgwick House, Kendal, banker, High Sheriff of Westmorland, 1854, born 1794, died 1866. = Fanny, daughter of Dr. McArthur, of Glasgow, mar. 1823.

Ann Wakefield, born 1797, mar. 1821, died 1876. = John Cropper, of Dingle Bank, Liverpool, born 1797, died 1874.
See page 64.

Edward William Wakefield, of Kendal, banker, born 1799, died 1858. = Susanna, eldest daughter of William Birkbeck, of Settle, Yorks, banker, mar. 1822.
See page 69.

Mary Wakefield, born 1824, mar. 1848, died 1855. = Rev. George Frederick Weston, M.A., Vicar of Crosby Ravensworth, 1848-87, died 1887.

Fanny Alison Wakefield, mar. 1860, died 1868. = James Cropper, of Eller Green, Kendal.
See pages 65, 71.

William Henry Wakefield, of Sedgwick House, Kendal, banker, born 1828, died 1889. = Augusta, daughter of late James Haggarty, U.S. Consul at Liverpool, mar. 1851.

Margaret Wakefield, mar. 1854. = Alfred Dudley Keightley, of Old Hall, Milnthorpe, died 1880.

Frances Elizabeth Weston, born 1849, mar. 1870. = Rev. George Herbert Lightfoot, M.A., Vicar of Pickering, Yorks.

Emily Margaret Weston, mar. 1880. = Constantine William Benson, Esq., of Milnthorpe.

John Wakefield Weston, born 1850, mar. 1890. = Kate, 3rd daughter of James R. Brougham.

Mary Keightley, died 1891.

Archibald Keightley, born 1859, mar. 1891, Julia Campbell, widow of —— Ver Planck.

John Prideaux Lightfoot, born 1871.

Robert Benson, born 1881. Mary W. Benson. Eleanor O. Benson.

Mary E. Weston.

Mary Augusta Wakefield.

Ruth Wakefield, mar. 1879, to Harvey Goodwin.
See page 73.

John Wakefield, of Sedgwick House, Kendal, banker, born 1858.

Jacob Wakefield, of Prizet, Kendal, J.P., Westmorland, born 1860. = Annie Wakefield, 2nd daughter of Jas. R. Brougham, mar. 1887.
See page 73.

Minnie Margaret Wakefield, mar. 1883, to Edward Augustus Arnold.
See page 73.

Agnes Wakefield, mar. 1893, to Thomas Atkinson Argles.

William Henry Wakefield, born 1870.

William Henry Wakefield.
1828-1889

Mrs W H Wakefield

Mary A Wakefield

Jacob Wakefield

W H Wakefield

(4) William Henry Wakefield, of Sedgwick House, Kendal, banker, J.P., D.L., Westmorland, High Sheriff 1871, born 18th May, 1828, died in the hunting field, 8th November, 1889; married 8th Aug., 1851, Augusta, daughter of late James Haggarty, Esq., U.S. Consul at Liverpool, and had 3 sons and 4 daughters:

(1) Mary Augusta Wakefield.

(2) Ruth Wakefield, married 23rd April, 1879, to Harvey, eldest son of Right Rev. Harvey Goodwin, D.D., Bishop of Carlisle, and has 2 sons and a daughter:

(1) Ruth Wakefield Goodwin, born at Eccles 8th February, 1880.

(2) Harvey Goodwin, born at Eccles 27th July, 1882.

(3) George Wycliffe Goodwin, born at Manchester, 3rd April, 1889.

(3) John Wakefield, of Sedgwick House, Kendal, banker, born 4th July, 1858.

(4) Jacob Wakefield, of Prizet, Kendal, J.P. Westmorland, High Sheriff, 1893, born 11th May, 1860; married 27th April, 1887, Annie Wakefield, 2nd daughter of James Rigg Brougham, Esq. (see page 68), and has a son:

William Henry Wakefield, born 6th Jan., 1891.

(5) Minnie Margaret Wakefield, married 2nd Aug., 1883, to Edward Augustus Arnold, Esq., of East Grinstead, Sussex (grandson of Dr. Arnold, of Rugby), and has 4 daughters:

(1) Margaret Trevenen Arnold, born 1st Sept., 1884.

(2) Mary Penrose Arnold, born 17th Oct., 1886.

(3) Ruth Wakefield Arnold, twin with

(4) Nancy Wordsworth Arnold, born 19th Dec., 1890.

(6) Agnes Wakefield, married 24th Jan., 1893, to Thomas Atkinson Argles, Esq., of Eversley, Milnthorpe; High Sheriff, Westmorland, 1891; M.A., Christ Church, Oxford, 1884; Barrister-at-Law, Lincoln's Inn, 1883.

(7) William Henry Wakefield, of New College, Oxford, born 28th May, 1870.

(5) Margaret Wakefield, born 6th Dec., 1829; married at Heversham 18th July, 1854, to Alfred Dudley Keightley, Esq., J.P., of Old Hall, Milnthorpe; he died 3rd August, 1880, leaving a son and daughter:

(1) Mary Keightley, born 8th Feb., 1856, died in New York, 11th June, 1891.

(2) Archibald Keightley, D.Med. Camb., born 19th April, 1859; married 25th Nov., 1891, Julia Wharton Lewis, widow of Philip W. Ver Planck, and daughter of Hon. James Campbell, late U.S. Minister at Stockholm.

(6) Agnes Wakefield, born 10th July, 1832, died young.

BISPHAM, OF YEALAND CONYERS.

JOSEPH BISPHAM, of Yealand Conyers, co. Lanc. (son of John Bispham and his wife Mary Bastwell, of Bickerstaffe, co. Lanc.), born 1678, iii. 17, died 1750, iii. 3, married at Yelland, 1699/1700, i. 6, Hannah, daughter of Robert Hubberstie, of Yealand, by his wife Ann Backhouse (see page 12); she died 1763, vi. 1, aged 88, having had 8 sons and a daughter:

(1) John Bispham, born 1700, xi. 2, died 1700, xii. 7.

(2) Benjamin Bispham, of Yelland Conyers, born there 1702, i. 31, died , married at Yelland 1727, v. 5, Sarah, daughter of Thomas Backhouse, of Yealand Redman, co. Lanc., yeoman (see page 14), she was buried 1731, vii. 20 (or viii. 29), and had at least a son and 3 daughters:

(1) Hannah Bispham, born 1727, xii. 19, died 1765, viii. 20.

(2) Thomas Bispham, of Bridgetown, West Jersey, a legatee under the Will of his uncle John Backhouse, of Hilderstone, 1763 (see page 81).

(3) John Bispham, senior (1763), of Mount Holly, Burlington Co., lumber merchant, father of:

John Bispham, junior, of Gloucester Co., also lumber merchant.

(4) Joseph, father of John, of Bridgetown, under age in 1763.

(3) Robert Bispham, born 1704, i. 27, died 1733, iv. 5.

(4) Joshua Bispham, of Manchester, born at Yelland, 1706, ii. 11 (query of Ayside, waller). Will dated 1766. By Mary his wife was father of:

Lawrence Bispham, born 1731, iv. 28.

(5) James Bispham, born at Yelland, 1708, iii. 29, died in London, 18th Nov., 1774.

(6) Mary Bispham, born at Yelland, 1710, iii. 13, died in Feb., 1778.

(7) Isaac Bispham, of Liverpool, cabinet maker, born at Yelland, 1712, vi. 17, died at Liverpool, 1793, ii. 4, married Eleanor, daughter of Isaac Hadwen, of ; she died at Liverpool, 21st or 22nd Sept., 1788, aged 71; having had 2 sons and 3 daughters, all born at Ormskirk:

(1) Sarah Bispham, died 6th Dec., 1826, aged 79; married 23rd Oct., 1777, to Isaac Cooke, of Manchester, after of Liverpool, who died there 22nd Aug., 1804, aged 56, having had 5 sons and 4 daughters.

(2) Hannah, died 1765, viii. 20, aged 15.

(3) Samuel Bispham, born 1752, viii. 12, died 1752, x. 26.

(4) Robert Bispham, born 1753, x. 15, died 1777, iv. 2.

(5) Mary Bispham, born 1761, iii. 3.

(8) Samuel Bispham, born at Yelland, 1715, i. 25, died 1743, viii. 18.

(9) Nathan Bispham, born at Yelland, 17 17/18, i. 6, died 1729, ii. 29.

WILLS AND INVENTORIES

WHICH ILLUSTRATE THE FOREGOING PEDIGREES.

Bond given by Robert Watson and Thomas Astley of Yealland, circa 1604, *as to goods, &c., of Robert Backus of Yealland.* (*See page* 12.)

[This document is very dilapidated and unreadable.]

Inventory of Goods, &c., of Richard Bacchus of Yealand Redman in the parish of Warton, taken 16*th Sept.*, 1640, *by Richard Bacchus, Richard Robinson, G. Watson, and Jo. Kilne.* (*See page* 12.)

£20. 11/-

Includes—

Oats & straw	2. 0. 0
Barley, &c.	3. 0. 0
Hay	10. 0
Beds & bedding	2. 0. 0
Apparal	13/-

Bond 24 Sept. 1640
given by Robert Fisher,
John Crosse
Robert Stable.

Will of John Backus (eldest), of Warton in the County of Lancaster, husbandman, 1641. *Proved*, 1651. (*See page* 12.)

[Three papers.]

JOHN BACKUS the eldest, of Warton, co. Lancaster, husbandman. Will dated 19 April, 1641. Proved 8 May, 1651. To be buried in Warton church. Inventory dated 10 May, 1650. = ELLIN, living 1641.

RICHARD, 1641.

JOHN, 1641.

"To be buryed in my parishe churche of Warton so neare to the place where my auncestors have been buryed as convenyently may be."

"To John Backus my sonne" the messuage bought of Robert Hutton of the inheritance of Robert Croft Gent. of the Yearly Value of 13/4 reserving "to Ellin now my wyef" a Moiety thereof during her widowhood, and acurding to the Custom of Warton.

"To said son John the Copyhold, held under the King, and had from John Burrowe and Robert Hutton, reserving also Moiety to wife.

"To Jane Backus the late daughter of Richard Backus late of Yealand redmain deceased" one lamb. (See page 12.)

Debts due to: Robert Croft £10. 16. 0, Isabel Turner £5. 8/-, Thomas Dawson £2. 3/-, Peter Wydder £2. 4/-, Jennett Stockdale £2. 3/-, Anthony Mason of Carneford 15/5, Elizabeth Crosser 21/7. Owing by—Robert Wallin 2/9.

Exors: Wife and Son.

Supervisors: Brother, Richard Backus, and Thomas Watson.

[Signed by the mark of John Backus eldest.]

Witnesses—
ROBERT DAWSON
CHRISTR TOMPSON
RIC- HEST.

Inventory of the Goods, &c., of Richard Backhus of Yealland Conyers. 1666.

(*See page* 12.)

RICHARD BACKHUS, of Yealland=ANNE, living
Conyers, co. Lancaster. Inventory 1667.
taken 6 May, 1666, £12 6s. 0d.
Bond dated 6 June, 1667.

Total amount £12. 6. 0.

including—
Bond £10. 16. 0
Apparel & (Purse?) 20/-
"One Arke" 10/-

Bond dated 6 June 1667, signed by Anne Backhouse of Yealand Conyers/
[Signed by—]
ANNE BACHUSE
Mark of ROBERT BACHUSE
CHR GUY.

Will of John Backhouse, of Yelland Redman, Co. Lancaster, Yeoman. 1690.

(*See page* 13.)

JOHN BACKHOUSE, of Yelland Redman, co. Lancaster, yeoman. Will dated 10 April, 1690. To be buried at Hilderston. Inventory taken 14 May, 1690. Bond dated 29 May, 1690. = SARAH, living 1690.

THOMAS, 1690. | JAMES, 1690. | (——) = JOHN CUMINGS | (——) = GEORGE ROBINSON.

"To the Poor Within the parish of Warton in the County aforesaid (the poor within Yelland Redman and Yelland Storrs only excepted) the sum of 20/- to be equally divided," and 10/- between the poor of the places excepted above.

"To Thomas Backhouse and James Backhouse my two Sones and John Cumings and George Robinson my two Sones in law," their heirs &c a third part of my Goods.

The other 2 parts being residue to "my loving wife Sarah Backhouse."

"I desire that my body may lie buryed att the burying place at Hilderston."

Mark of John Backhouse.

Witnesses:—EDWARD KILNER
JOHN SMITH
RICHARD LANCASTER.

Inventory 14 May 1690.
£69-7-0
Cow and 3 heifers £10. 10. 0. Marc £2. 15. 0.

Bond 29 May 1690 by Sarah Backhouse of Yelland.

Bond given by Mary Backhouse, the relict of Richard Backhouse of Yealland, in the parish of Warton, deceased, and Robert Backhous the son, dated 23rd Dec., 1696, to properly administer, &c. (*See page* 12.)

RICHARD BACKHOUSE, of Yealland, par. Warton, co. Lancaster. Bond dated 23 Dec., 1696. = MARY, living 1696.

ROBERT.

Witnesses—
J[s] LAMBERT.
— CHAMBERS.

[Signed by]
ROBERT BACKHOUS.

Will of James Backhouse of Yealand Conyers, Co. Lancaster, husbandman. 1697. (*See page* 14.)

JAMES BACKHOUSE, of Yealand Conyers, co. Lancaster, husbandman. Will dated 3 May, 1697. Admon. 3 July, 1697. Inventory taken 16 June, 1697, £171 12*s*. = JENNETT, living 1697.

WILLIAM, 1697, youngest son. | SARAH, 1697.

To Jennett Backhouse. She to pay debts, and to look after Tuition of the children.

He left one third each to "Wife Jennett"; "William Backhouse my youngest son" and to "Sarah Backhouse my daughter."

Wife to be Exōr.

(signed)
JAMES BACKHOUSE.

Witnesses—
GEORGE GODSALVE.
JOHN COWAN Jun[r].
WILLIAM WAITHMAN.

Bonds dated 3 July 1697, given by Jennet Backhouse, widow, Nathaniel Huberstey of Yealand and George Godsalve.

(she signs)
JONNET BACKHOUSE.

Inventory 16 June 1697 £171. 12/- includes Bond of James Backhouse & Tho[s] Kilner for £105.

Will of Thomas Backhouse of Yealand Redman, in the parish of Warton, Co. Lancaster, Yeoman. 1729. (*See page* 13.)

THOMAS BACKHOUSE, of Yealand Redmaine, par. Warton, co. Lancaster, yeoman. Will dated 20 May, 1729. Proved 1 Oct., 1729. Inventory taken 18 June, 1729, £125 15*s*. =

JOHN, 1729. | SARAH, 1729. = BENJAMIN BISPHAM.

Appoints son John executor.

"Unto my loving daughter Sarah, the wife of Benjamin Bispham," dwelling house, barn, land, &c. "wherein Margaret ffoster now liveth," with one Croft lying on the east side containing one acre; also

half an acre on the west side; one close called Salter mier Close containing one acre 3 roods; also 3 roods in the town field called Sinder barrow also one rood adjoining. Also parcels of Moss ground in the White moss. Also one dale of Moss in the place called Little Dales & two brakindales lying upon that part of Yealand Common called Yealand high. Also two cattle gats of Grassing in Hungerhill within the liberties of the town of Lupton Co. Westmorland which is freehold.

To daughter Sarah a chest in Middle Chamber.

Residue to son John "my heir at law," Exör.

Supervisors & overseers:—My Cousins William Backhouse of Over Kellet and Edward Cuming of Hilderston.

Witnesses:
HENRY CLARKESON.
JENNET BURROW.
EDWARD CUMMINGE.

Bond dated 1st October 1729 of John Backhouse, Yeoman, & John Doe, the said John to pay debts, &c.

Signed:—
JOHN BACKHOUSE.

Inventory taken 18th June 1729 by John Beetham, Joseph Parker, Edw. Cuminge.

Total £125. 15/-

includes:—

Purse and apparel	£10
Sheep and Wood	£5 12/-
3 Work-Horses	£10.
4 Kine, 2 Oxen, 6 Steers, 5 heifers	= £48.

Debts owing to testator 16/6.

Will, &c., of Robert Backhouse, of Yealand Conyers, Yeoman. 1728.

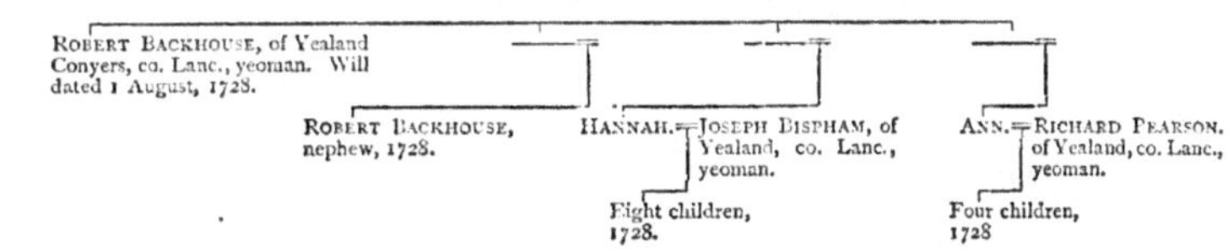

The last will of Robert Backhouse of Yealand Conyers Co. Lanc. yeoman. I give my messuage and dwelling house &c with all lands and tenements to my nephew Robert Backhouse his heirs and assigns. To the eight children of my niece Hannah the wife of Joseph Bispham twenty pounds between them to the said Joseph Bispham five shillings. To the four children of my niece Ann wife

of Richard Pearson twenty pounds between them, to the said Richard five shillings. To Agnes Stephenson my servant twenty pounds with all "quick" household and husbandry goods. Nieces Hannah and Anne Executrices to whom the residue is bequeathed. Dated *1st August 1728.* Witnessed by Lawrence Johnson Margaret Johnson Jno Backhouse.

Inventory of the goods &c of Robert Backhouse. Total £176 10s 10½ apprized by John Backhouse Robert Watson John Collison, Henry Rowlandson.

Bond of Joseph Bispham of Yealand parish of Warton in co. Lancr yeoman and Richard Pearson of Yealand yeoman for £500, dated *17 Augt 1728.*

Will, &c., of John Backhouse, of Hornby, yeoman. 1739.

WILLIAM, of Kellet. | JOHN BACKHOUSE, of Hornby, co. Lanc., yeoman. Will dated 19 Nov., 1739, proved 15 Dec., 1740. = MARGARET. | JOHN AIREY, of Kendal.

MARY. JAMES. JOHN. MARGARET.

I John Backhouse of Hornby co. Lancaster yeoman. To wife Margaret and children Mary James John & Margaret Backhouse the whole of my goods effects & personal estate equally between them. Brother William Backhouse of Kellet and Brother in law John Airey of Kendall executors in trust to make an inventory and dispose of effects.

Witnessed the *19th Nov. 1739* by John Varley "Jon" Thornton.

Probate *15 Decr 1740* to John Airey. *10 Jany 1740* Wm Backhouse the other executor appeared and affirmed to the will.

Bond of John Airey of Kirkby Kendall co. Westmoreland tobacconist and William Backhouse of Kellet parish of Bolton by the Sands co. Lanc. Flaxman for £600 dated *15th Decr 1740.*

Will of William Backhouse, of Over Kellett, Dealer in yarn. 1761.

WILLIAM BACKHOUSE, of Over Kellett, dealer in yarn. Will dated 3 March, 1761, proved 6 June following. = AGNES.

JAMES. WILLIAM.

After debts residue to his wife Agnes for life remainder to his children at the discretion of his wife. Executors his wife and sons James and William. Dated 6 day of third month called March 1761, proved 6 June following.

Admon. Jane Backhouse, of Lancaster. 1763.

JOHN BACKHOUSE. Admon.=JANE BACKHOUSE, formerly
18 Feb., 1763. DODGSON. See page 16.

John Backhouse & John Barrow, merchants and Thomas Calvert, innholder give bond to administer to effects of Jane Backhouse formerly Dodgson of Lancaster dec[d], *18 Feb., 1763.*

Will of John Backhouse, of Hilderstone, Yeoman. 1763.

JOSEPH BISPHAM,=HANNAH HUBBERSTIE.
of Bickerstaffe. See page 83.

BENJAMIN BISPHAM.=SARAH BACKHOUSE. JOHN BACKHOUSE.
Mar. 1727, bur. 1731. Will 1779.

THOMAS, 1763. £20.

JOSEPH.=
JOHN BISPHAM, 1763. £20.

JOHN BISPHAM, sen., of Mount Holly, Burlington co., lumber merchant. £20.=
JOHN BISPHAM, jun., of Gloucester co., lumber merchant.

John Backhouse of Hilderstone, yeoman maketh his will as follows:—

I give to my cousin John Cumming of Hilderstone aforesaid yeoman my freehold messuage & tenement consisting of dwelling house outhouses gardens orchards fronts & foulds &[c] lying in Yelland Redman & Yelland Storrs also the dwelling house Backside Moss & appurtenances at Throng End in Yelland Storrs for ever chargeable with the following legacies:—

To my two nephews Thomas and John Bispham brothers now resident at Bridgetown in West Jersey to each £20 also I give to their brother Joseph's son John Bispham now a minor at Bridgetown £20. I give to my cousin Hannah now wife of Thomas Pearson of Pool Bank in Witherslack Westmorland £20. All my goods & chattels &[c] I give to my cousin John Cumming whom I appoint Executor.

Dated *26 Dec 1763.*

Witnesses, Thomas Beakbane, Thomas Backhouse, John Bradley, Edward Cumming.

Proved at Richmond by John Cumming the Exör *19 June 1779.*

Will of Richard Backhouse, of Throng End, husbandman. 1764.

From the Hilderstone Papers, penes Edward C. Backhouse.

RICHARD BACKHOUSE, of Throng End, in Yelland Storrs. Will dated 4 Feb., 1764, not proved. =

THOMAS — WILLIAM. — ELIZABETH. MARY. — MARGARET. ANN.

Richard Backhouse of Throng End in Yelland Storrs par. of Warton co. Lanc. husbandman made his will as follows :—

First I give to John Cumming of Hilderstone, yeoman my enclosure or Backside near a Backhous & Dwelling house belonging to John Backhouse called Throng End together with a *Moss side* chargeable with £30 to the following uses. To my eldest son Thomas Backhouse the sum of 1s if he appear to demand it personally of the said John Cumming which is to be in full his part of my estate. To my younger son William Backhouse who hath some natural incapacities, I give the yearly interest of the said £30, *i.e.* £1. 5. 0. yearly if that is sufficient besides what he earns by his industry to keep him alive, otherwise I wish a yearly sum to be taken from the £30 as may be wanted. If any or all of the £30 be left I will it be divided among my daughters viz. Elizabeth, Mary, Margaret & Ann share & share alike; also I give to my son William and daughters all my household goods, credits, chattels & I do make my son William and my daughters my executors.

Dated *4 Feb. 1764.* Not proved.

Witnesses, DOROTHY JACKSON
JOHN JACKSON
EDWARD HAYTON.

Receipt given for £1. 5. 0. by W. B. 21 Nov. 1765 to 26 Nov. 1781.

Note to preceding will.—At the Court Baron of John Warren & Thomas Preston, Esq[rs], & Chris. Guy Lords of the Manor of Yelland Redman, Yelland Coniers, & Yelland Storrs cum membris held at Yelland Storrs 20 June 34 Charles II. A.D. 1682. The following were tenants :—

Yelland Storrs, Thomas Backhouse.

Yelland Redman, John Backhouse. John B., jun[r].

Yelland Coniers, Robert Backhouse. Rich. B.

Among the names of the Jury for making enquiry & presenting &c. were John Backhouse, jun[r] & Robert Backhouse. The Jury found—"John Backhouse whole tenant according to the custom of the manor, of one close yearly rent 3 by conveyance from Robert More now deceased, dated 5 Feb. 1680."

Will, &c., of John Hubbersty, of Yealand Conyers, yeoman. 1697.

JOHN HUBBERSTY, of Yealand Conyers, co. Lanc. Will dated 21 June, 1697, proved 8 Oct. following. To be buried in parish church or churchyard of Warton. = AGNES.

THOMAS. ELIZABETH. MARGARET.

I John Hubberstey of Yealand Conyers co. Lancaster. To be buried in the parish church or churchyard of Warton. To my son Thomas Hubbersty one table one "chist" &c and full satisfaction of his childs part or portion of my goods. Remainder to my wife and my two daughters equally between them. Executrix wife Agnes & two daughters Elizabeth and Margaret. Dated *21st June 1697*. Witnessed by "Johnathn" Watson, George Beethome Chrifr Guy.

Inventory of the goods &c of John Hubersty of Yealand Conyers apprised by William Hugginson, Henry Simpkinson, George Hodgson and Nathan Hubbersty, *6 July 1697*. Total £100.2.2. Debts £80.

Bond of Agnes Hubberstey Henry Simpkinson and Thomas Hadwen both of Carneforth parish of Warton co. Lanc. yeoman for £50. Dated *8th October 1697*. Witnessed by Thomas Backhouse & Robt Heblethwaite.

Probate to Agnes the widow *8th Oct. 1697*. The testator is described in the grant as yeoman.

Will, &c., of Nathan Hubberstie, of Yelland Conyers, yeoman. 1709.

NATHAN HUBBERSTIE, of Yelland Conyers, parish of Warton, co. Lanc., yeoman. Will dated 25 April, 1709. = MARY.

HANNAH. See page 81. = JOSEPH BISPHAM. of Bickerstaffe.

BENJAMIN. ROBERT. JOSHUA. JAMES

I Nathan Huberstie of Yelland Conyers parish of Warton co. Lancaster yeoman. To wife Mary & heirs messuage and tenement closes &c in the parish of Grasingame. To friends Robert Chamber of Sidgwicke co. Westmoreland tanner. John Moore of Hayle in Lancashire yeoman Anthony Stonay of Crumock parish of Clapham co. York, and brother-in-law "Johnathan" Thornton of Deep Clough parish of Caton co. Lanc. all customary messuages known as Thursgill & Gillgarth parish of Horton in Ribelsdale co. York in trust, to sell the same to the best advantage, invest the proceeds and pay the issues and profits to Mary the wife during her life. After her death the investments to be sold and divided between nephews Robert Joshua and James Bispham, the younger sons of my sister Hannah wife of Joseph Bispham of Bickerstaffe equally. . . . . Said nephews to have £100 each out of the personal estate on reaching the age of twenty one. To friends William and Robert Waithman of Lindeth £20. To the poor of Yellands £1. 10. 0. To nephew Benjamin Bispham eldest son of sister Hannah 10s thereby debarring him from further advantage, to brother and sister in law William and Ann Thornton 10s each. To coz. Thomas Huberstie 10s. Remainder to wife Mary who is

appointed executrix. Dated *25th April 1709.* Witnessed by Robert Backhouse junr. Richd Backhouse, Robert Barker.

Inventory (in duplicate) of the goods &c of Nathan Huberstie yeoman apprised the *20th May 1709* by Robert Backhouse, Robt Chamber Jno Moore Anthony Stonay.

Total 395. 16. 6. Debts owing by him £206. 0. 0. remains £189. 16. 6.

Bond of Mary Hubbersty of Yealand Conyers widow and John Backhouse of Yealand Conyers yeoman for £1000. Dated *19 March 1714.*

Bond of Joseph Bispham of Yelland Conyers yeoman and John Bispham of Bickerstaffe parish of Ormeskirke yeoman, dated *6 Sept. 1716* for securing the proper maintenance and education of Robert, Joshua and James Bispham the children of Joseph Bispham.

INDEX.

MATCHES AND CONTEMPORARIES.

1894.

(*An asterisk denotes a Portrait.*)

Index.

Index.

M

Index.

CHISWICK PRESS:—C. WHITTINGHAM AND CO., TOOKS COURT, CHANCERY LANE.

26

Lightning Source UK Ltd.
Milton Keynes UK
UKHW050624310822
408116UK00008B/703

9 789354 413964